W9-BJM-063

10 Easy Writing Lessons That Get Kids Ready for Writing Assessments

Proven Ways to Raise Your Students' Scores on the State Performance Assessments in Writing

by Mary C. Rose

SCHOLASTIC PROFESSIONAL BOOKS

New York • Toronto • London • Auckland • Sydney

DEDICATION

To Tom, my very best friend

ACKNOWLEDGEMENTS

To Ms. Donna J. Smith, Dr. Jacquelyn Hughes, Dr. Lee Baldwin, and Mr. John Rowland for assessment expertise and for believing in me from the very start. I'd also like to thank Lauren Tarshis, and editors Wendy Murray, Camilla Franck, and Tom Becker.

Scholastic Inc. grants teachers the right to photocopy the reproducibles from this book for classroom use.
No other part of this book may be reproduced in whole or in part, or stored in a retrieval system, or transmitted in any form
or by any means, electronic, mechanical, photocopying, recording, or otherwise, without permission of the publisher.
For permission, write to Scholastic Professional Books, 555 Broadway, New York, NY, 10012.

Front cover design by Kathy Massaro

Cover photograph by Oi Pin Chan

Interior design by Sydney Wright

Interior photographs on pages 6, 9, 31, 39, 49, 57, 63, 83 by Oi Pin Chan;
page 98, by Glen Mariconda; all other photos courtesy of the author.

ISBN 0-439-05010-3
Copyright © 1999 by Mary C. Rose, all rights reserved.
Printed in USA

Contents

Foreword

*I*n the 1992-93 school year the state of Florida instituted the Florida Writes! Assessment (FWA) for grades 4, 8, and 10. I was teaching fourth grade at the time, and I was not concerned about my students' scores! No, not me. My kids did a lot of writing, from process writing to journals, letters, reports—they even had their own newspaper. I was not concerned about any assessment of my students' writing ability.

The FWA is scored on a scale of 1-6. That first year my class score was a 1.6. I was horrified and shocked. There must surely be something wrong with the test! I had been so confident that my students would score at least a 3 or even a 4 on that test.

I have spent the last several years working on improving the Florida Writes! Assessment scores for my classroom and more recently for the entire Orange County Public School District. What I have learned has been a combination of my own intuition about students and how they learn; the result of many classes and workshops intended to teach me about writing skills; and the synthesis of all of this into the guidelines put forth by the FWA. I have realized that the FWA is not vastly different from the writing assessments being mandated in several other states. Because of this, I have decided to share with others not only what I have learned about the teaching of writing and how to get an intermediate-elementary student to write effectively, but also how to teach this in such a way as to raise test scores for your students. The lessons in this book have been used extensively by many teachers in Florida with remarkable results—virtually every school using these lessons has shown improvement in test scores and several schools have raised their scores by as much as one whole point on a six point scale.

Many of the student examples you see in this book are from the fourth grade class I taught in 1998-1999. They are representative of students from several cultures, languages and levels of ability. I long ago tired of seeing wonderful, incredible examples of student writing in writing instruction books. I hope you will find that these are more relevant—because they are real writings from real kids!

Introduction

*A*ll across America classroom teachers are facing the prospect of administering more and more tests to students at virtually every grade level. This trend will surely gain momentum as states continue to place even greater emphasis on test scores, sometimes relying on these numbers for teacher evaluation, student promotion, district ratings, and even school funding. At the same time, many states are also changing the ways tests are administered, the way tests are scored, and the skills students are expected to demonstrate. Everyone seems to be working harder than ever; unfortunately, students' scores do not always reflect these efforts. Nowhere is this more true than in the teaching of writing.

Our writing lessons frequently center on free-style writing and journals. Free-style writing is wonderful—it allows students to be creative and encourages writing as a "fun" discipline—but it doesn't necessarily focus on the nuts and bolts of writing: creating stories that have a beginning, middle, and end and contain sufficient dialogue, character development, and description. We also emphasize creativity at the expense of some crucial elements of good writing, such as organizational skills, focused writing, grammar, and spelling. These elements of good writing do not just naturally occur; they need to be taught. If they are not stressed early on, many students will continue making the same mistakes over and over, convinced that creative ideas alone make for good writing.

As educators, we have to cope with change on a regular basis. We take classes and workshops to keep abreast of new techniques, new technologies, new challenges in our classrooms. As a consequence, we often don't take—or have!—the time to

brush up on old skills. So while writing teachers can recognize good writing when they see it, they may have difficulty identifying exactly what makes the writing good. Consequently they cannot show their students the strategies and tools writers use to create good writing.

With state testing, most of us are at a disadvantage, as we are unfamiliar with the criteria by which our students are scored. Once we understand the "language of the test," we are better able to help our students improve their scores. Terms for assessing writing vary, but basically each state is looking for the same elements. In this book, I cover what "organization," "voice," "extension," and "elaboration" mean to the readers that will be scoring their students' work.

About 30 states currently require a student writing assessment, and most of these have a very similar format. Students are given a set amount of time to read and respond to a prompt (or writing suggestion). Prompts are either expository (the student is asked to explain something), narrative (the student tells a fiction or nonfiction story), or persuasive (the student writes an essay to persuade someone to act or change an opinion about a given topic). A few states offer students a second sitting in which to complete a final draft of their work, but most often it is the rough draft that is scored.

The student work is usually scored holistically, meaning that the essay is judged as a complete piece of work. Points are not awarded for individual skills such as spelling, punctuation, description, and so on. This scoring is based on a general scoring rubric, which outlines basic features that an essay should contain in order to reach the various scoring levels. Most student papers are read at least two times and are independently scored. While consensus is not necessary, those papers with a wide gap in the two scores are read a third time before a final score is assigned. Student scores are reported on a scale of 1-4 or 1-6, with a 1 being the lowest score. (Some papers are also rated as "Unscoreable.")

While states use different terms for the elements of writing, they are all looking for the same criteria. In the chart below, the most commonly used terms are defined, along with other terms used by various states to describe the same aspect of writing. Despite the differences, it is easy to see that all of the assessments value the same writing skills. From Vermont to Kentucky to Texas to Washington, everywhere I looked, each state recognizes what good writing skills look like and scores its papers accordingly.

The Elements of Good Writing—and a High Score

The following criteria are essential in a student's work for a high writing assessment score:

Focus ~

This is considered the most crucial element of writing—staying on the topic and writing about what the prompt instructed the student to address. Many students tend to wander off the topic or misunderstand the prompt, thus obtaining a poor score. This aspect is also called purpose, prompt, topic, subject, key event, or main event.

Organization ~

It should be evident to the reader that the author began with a plan in mind and systematically developed each of his ideas. A good essay or story includes an introduction and closing. Narrative pieces have a distinct beginning, middle, and end. Expository and persuasive work should include definite reasons or steps to take. This aspect is also called format, plan, or method.

Support ~

This is usually the most difficult of the skills for young students to master. Support includes many things, from command of the language to voice, style, tone, and detail. It is here that the student discusses her topic sentences and fully develops the main ideas presented in the piece. This aspect is also called details, description, elaboration, or extensions.

Conventions of Print ~

Conventions are all of those things that make the written language friendly to the reader, such as following the accepted rules of punctuation, capitalization, indentation, and spelling. This aspect is also called usage, mechanics, or grammar.

All four of these criteria are developed within each lesson in this book. This is considered a "gradual release" method of teaching, meaning that students begin to write with a lot of structure and, as they gradually increase their knowledge and mastery of new skills, they receive less guidance from the teacher. The basic steps are repeated lesson after lesson, each one offering a few new skills. Each lesson helps the student reach a new level of ability. The book is divided into 10 lessons; please try to do them in order. There is also a "bonus lesson" and a final section of exercises you can do throughout the school year. The book also includes strategies for:

◆ infusing these key writing skills into student work across the curriculum

◆ applying the four criteria to report writing

◆ understanding the difference between expository, narrative, and persuasive essays

◆ teaching students to use transitions, a variety of sentence structures, elaboration, and description

◆ improving students' spelling and proofreading skills

◆ turning the writing projects into great bulletin board displays

Most teachers and schools that have used these writing lessons have dramatically improved students' scores on state assessments, often raising them as much as a whole point in a school year. The approach has been very successful in even the most "at risk" schools, where many students are functioning far below grade level. However, it's important to remember that raising test scores is just a by-product of great instruction. These students may get higher writing scores, but they also have learned a valuable lifelong skill of being able to organize their thoughts and put them on paper for reports, letters, essays, and recreational writing.

I hope that by using the methods in this book, your classroom will be full of budding authors who actually enjoy writing. In the meantime, if your test scores go up, perhaps one of the many pressures that teachers feel will be lessened for you. Good luck with your writing and with your writing assessments.

Introducing the Five-Paragraph Essay

Skills	Indentation, paragraphing, use of the colon, commas between words in a series, use of capitals and periods, writing an expository essay
Time Allotted	Four to five 40-minute writing sessions. (Includes illustrations and display.)
Materials	Markers and chart paper for teacher use (about 6 sheets) Paper and pencil for students Two sheets of 9" x 12" construction paper for each child (optional) Crayons or colored pencils for student use One brown paper bag for each child to take home

A classroom of writers

The best way to teach a child to write is by having him or her write! Simple enough. But how about getting them to write effectively? We don't simply tell our students, "write a great story about . . ." or "give me a really interesting essay on . . ." and expect good writing to appear. If only it were that easy! Unfortunately, we can't expect a nine year old to do what many adults have difficulty doing: create a full-blown essay that is focused on an assigned topic, organized, and fully developed with similes, alliteration, description, elaborations, and so on and remember all the rules of writing that he is just now mastering.

This first writing lesson, designed for the beginning of a school year, provides a model for children to follow, a subject they know and love (themselves), and a framework within which they will create a wonderful essay about the objects that are important to them. This is a very basic lesson: The student gets first-hand experience in writing his own title, introduction, topic sentences, extensions, and closing—five paragraphs in all. This same framework is used for future assignments, so that this type of essay writing eventually becomes automatic for students.

This first writing lesson may take as long as a week; when completed, the work can be shared and celebrated in some way, such as a read-aloud to the rest of the class, a display at Parent's Open House, or a bulletin board.

Be sure to follow the steps outlined below, even if you are teaching middle school or advanced elementary school students. If students are already familiar with the skills involved, then the writing lesson will be easy for them, but even the advanced student may learn something new—such as when to begin a new paragraph!

Lesson 1

> **Prompt**   Tell interesting things about yourself

Preparation

1. Familiarize yourself with the model essay on page 19, and the sample student essay on page 16.

2. Collect three objects that express something important about you and put them in a paper bag.

3. Write your own essay, using the model essay as a guide. Notice that paragraphs 2, 3, and 4 each begin with a sentence that names the object and are followed by two sentences about it. Please follow this model precisely, avoiding the temptation to add more details or description.

4. Copy your essay onto chart paper or an overhead transparency. (Charts often work better, as they can be hung up and used as a reference.)

5. Supply a brown paper lunch bag for each student.

6. Photocopy your parent note about the assignment and attach a copy to each lunch bag. (See sample next page.)

Centreal, Carly, and Sharika hard at work

Presenting the lesson~Day One

Keeping your paper bag closed, read aloud the first paragraph (introduction) of your essay. Before reading paragraph 2, remove from the bag the item it describes and then hold it up while you read. Do this for the second and third objects. Close the bag with a flourish before reading aloud the closing. Then ask students the following questions to stimulate discussion:

◆ Look at the essay. Can you tell by looking at it when I stopped talking about each new item? (Yes. Each item is a separate paragraph, indicated by an indentation.)

◆ What does the colon signal? (a list follows)

◆ When I was reading the essay, did you notice when the bag was closed? (During the introduction and the closing. At this point, you can explain to your students that the introduction presents to readers what the essay is about, while the closing serves to sum up for the reader.)

◆ Can you name the topic of this essay? (The topic is the teacher's favorite things.)

Distribute lunch bags to your students. Ask them to return them to school tomorrow with three objects that will tell everyone something about them. Tell students that they will be writing a five-paragraph essay about themselves.

Discuss the kinds of objects that might be appropriate to bring to school (small items that fit in the bag, nothing with great monetary value, no irreplaceable or breakable items, things that truly tell something about the writer). Tell students that they can bring a drawing, photograph, or small toy to represent something they cannot actually put in the bag.

Dear Parents,

Attached to this note is a brown paper bag. Your child's homework tonight is to find three of his or her favorite things to put into this bag. These three things should tell the class about your child's personality or favorite activities.

Please do not allow your child to bring in large, breakable, or expensive items. If your child has a special item that is not appropriate to bring to school, please help your child find a drawing, photograph or small toy that would represent that item. Everything that your child brings must fit into the bag. Your child should only bring three items.

Thank you so much for your assistance with this project.

Sincerely,

Sample letter to parents.

Day Two

Put up your essay and read it aloud, repeating the removal of items from the brown paper bag just like yesterday. See if students can begin to see how the two essays (theirs and yours) will be alike. Since it is early in the school year, it is a good idea to walk your students through the first two or three essays—don't worry, they'll be writing independently soon enough!

On a chalkboard or chart paper, write "My" for students to copy onto their papers. Mention the fact that this first word is indented, meaning that a new paragraph is started. Circulate around the room to make sure that each and every child has indented and capitalized that first word. Then write the rest of the first sentence ("My name is _____.") and have students copy this and add their names.

Add the second sentence ("I am _____ years old"). Ask your students to copy that and add their ages. Then write the third sentence ("I think school is _____"). Encourage your students to think up creative words that can go in this blank. You can accept almost anything here from "boring" to "wonderful," but try to help students use a variety of descriptors.

Finally, write the fourth sentence ("In my bag I have these things:") and ask students to copy it.

When everyone in the class has reached this stopping place, point out that you have used a colon (:) after the word "things." This indicates that the writer is about to make a list. Ask your students to check their own papers to be sure that this was done. Now ask them

Zana creates an illustration for her activity.

to write down one thing from their bags and then make a comma. Then tell students to write down the second thing in their bags and make another comma. Now write the word "and," and have them list the third thing from their bags. Now add a period. (You can refer to your model if students become confused.) Inform the class that they have just finished the first paragraph of the essay. Reread your essay and compare the two. Can they guess what will happen next?

Have students remove the first object from their paper bag and set it on their desks. Then demonstrate where on the paper they should place the next word, the letter: I. (Make sure that everyone indents to begin this next section. Just saying to "indent" is rarely enough! Circulate the room to make sure students have indented and have used a capital I.) Write on the chart or chalkboard:

I brought a _____ because _____.

In the first blank, students should write the first thing that they wrote when making the list above and then finish the sentence. Then have your students write two more sentences about that object. (Because it is something "near and dear" to their hearts, this usually isn't too difficult!) These additional sentences are called *extensions*. They support the topic sentence by giving more information about it. You can prompt with the following questions:

Where did you get it?
Where do you keep it?
When do you play with or use the item?
Who gave it to you?
Do you have more like it at home?

Getting to this point usually takes one whole 40-minute writing period. If it has taken you that long, please stop! Collect the papers, and let your students know that they will continue the assignment on another day. And don't worry about going slowly. This first lesson is the most important of all of the writing lessons.

Day Three

Once again put up and read aloud your essay, repeating the removal of objects from the bag. Then return papers to your students, and have them put their paper bags on their desks. Allow some time for each student to silently reread his work. Ask if they can predict what will happen next.

Have the students remove the second object from their bags. On the chalkboard or chart paper, write:

I also brought a _____. I brought it because _____.

Students write the names of the second item on their lists. Then they finish the "because" sentence and add one or two sentences about the object. Watch for those indentations!!

Now the students remove the third object and write:

Last of all, I have a _____. I brought it because _____.

The students finish the sentence and add two more sentences about the object. Do they see a pattern emerging? Take a minute and discuss what has happened in their essays. Compare it to yours.

If your students are very inexperienced writers, writing about these two objects may have taken up most of your writing instructional time. If this is the case, pause so they can reread their essays from the beginning and write the closing on day four.

If you have time to complete this project on day three, instruct students to put all three objects back into their bags. Then allow them time to reread what they have written. See if they can guess what part is missing. With all of the bags "closed" they need a "closing" to their stories. You can create your own essay closing or use the following:

I enjoyed telling you all about me. I want to read about other kids in our room. I am looking forward to a great school year at _____ Elementary School!

Your students have just written their first five-paragraph essay. They went slowly and laboriously through this first writing because it sets the stage for writing projects the whole year through.

Do not throw this essay away or even send it home. You may use it for a display, but be sure to keep it, as you will need it for a future writing lesson outlined in this book. Do not grade this first attempt at writing the five-paragraph essay.

Here is Robert's illustration for his essay.

Day Four

If your students finished writing on Day three, then on Day Four have them create a self-portrait on some heavy construction paper. Use an identical sheet as a back and staple the writing pages inside to create a book. Staple these onto a bulletin board along with the words "Look Who's in Fourth Grade," or (if they don't write their names on the front of the book) "Guess Who's in Fourth Grade?"

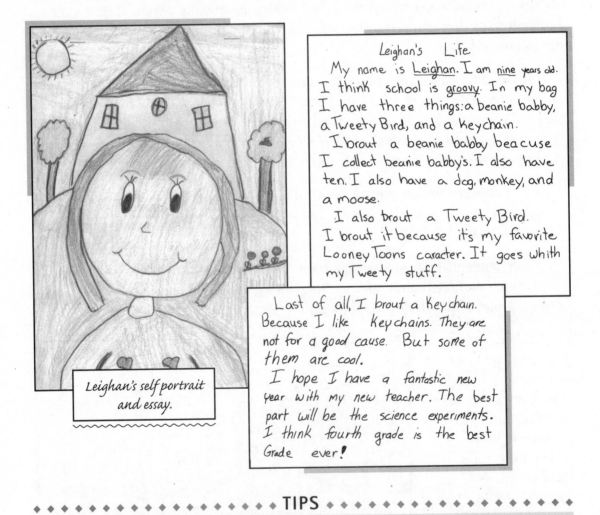

Leighan's self portrait and essay.

Leighan's Life
My name is <u>Leighan</u>. I am <u>nine</u> years old. I think school is <u>groovy</u>. In my bag I have three things: a beanie babby, a Tweety Bird, and a keychain.

I brout a beanie babby beacuse I collect beanie babby's. I also have ten. I also have a dog, monkey, and a moose.

I also brout a Tweety Bird. I brout it because it's my favorite Looney Toons caracter. It goes whith my Tweety stuff.

Last of all, I brout a keychain. Because I like keychains. They are not for a good cause. But some of them are cool.

I hope I have a fantastic new year with my new teacher. The best part will be the science experiments. I think fourth grade is the best Grade ever!

····· TIPS ·····

- Do not assume that your students will return the following day with their little bags full of goodies. Schedule the second and third writing sessions a day or two after the initial presentation so that everyone will have their items in their bags. Allow students who have not brought items to write or draw or glue pictures onto three index cards that can represent their three items.

- On Day Four some children might begin drawing self-portraits while others are completing their essays. Try to circulate and offer individual help to those students who are still writing. Refer to the previous list of questions to motivate students to continue. Remember: At this time you are not seeking perfection or long, elaborate sentences. Those students who need more time to complete the writing can do the illustrations as homework. All writing for these exercises must be done in class.

- For Parent's Open House night put the books around the room, and challenge each parent to find their child's essay without opening the book. Then provide them time to read their child's work.

- Save these essays, and reread them just before parent conferences. They can remind you of some interesting things about each child and may offer starting points for talking with parents.

- Keep these essays all year long. You will need them for a future lesson, and they can also serve to show how your students are developing as writers during school year.

◆ Variations ◆

Instead of writing about three objects in a paper bag, students can bring in pictures of their favorite foods and glue them onto paper plates. You can staple their essays to the back of the plates and arrange the completed plates on a bulletin board so that they look like they are around a picnic table. Or have students bring in photos of three favorite toys to write about. For the bulletin board, glue the pictures onto construction paper that has been decorated to look like toy boxes, or make one huge brown toy box, attach pictures of their favorites, and display the essays below. Remember to create your own essay to use as a model.

Student writing can go on and on without a new paragraph being introduced. When writing about three items, students have a physical representation of when to "paragraph." You will see this format repeated throughout the book (although we will not be using a paper bag).

◆ Spelling and Grammar Practice ◆

Create four charts in your classroom. Put one of the following chunks on the top of each chart.

- - tion   - - ture   - - ough   - - ight

Challenge students to think of words that contain any of these spelling stumpers. Have students write their words under the correct heading. Keep the chart posted so students can continue to add to the lists. (A small Post-it™ note on the desk can be used to record words they find during a reading lesson so that the lesson is not interrupted.)

You could just purchase these charts, but letting the students find and record the words is very important. This makes the charts "theirs" and students are more likely to use them for references in their writing if they are the ones who have created them. (If you are working with exceptional education students or very young students, introduce these four charts one at a time, several days apart.)

Now that students have completed their first essays, they are ready to go forward. Remember to keep your model essay posted somewhere in the classroom and refer to it often so that students begin to see the similarities between it and the next project. Even though the first project is expository and the second is narrative, the format and the concepts are the same.

Three Favorite Things

I have enjoyed being your reading teacher so far this year. I brought this bag to help tell you about me. In the bag I have three things: a puzzle piece, a seashell, and a small book.

I brought a puzzle piece because I collect antique wooden puzzles. Most of them are almost 100 years old. I keep them in heart-shaped boxes.

I also brought a seashell. I brought it because I love to scuba dive. Mr. Rose and I go diving one or two times a year. We are careful not to hurt living things under the water.

Last of all, I have a book. I brought it because I love to read. Usually I read mysteries. I also read lots of science magazines.

Now you know three important things about me. We will have lots of fun learning together this year, but first I want to know at least three things about you!

10 Easy Writing Lessons That Get Kids Ready for Writing Assessments
Scholastic Professional Books

LESSON 2

Using the Graphic Organizer to Plan for Writing

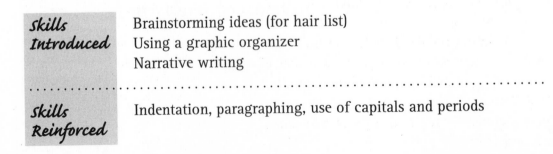

Skills Introduced	Brainstorming ideas (for hair list) Using a graphic organizer Narrative writing
Skills Reinforced	Indentation, paragraphing, use of capitals and periods

Time Allotted	Three-to-four 40-minute writing sessions (includes illustrations and display)
Materials	Markers and chart paper for teacher use (about 6 sheets) Paper and pencil for students Two 8" x 12" sheets of construction paper per child (optional) Roll of plastic wrap (optional) Crayons or colored pencils

Now that students have had some experience with writing an expository piece, they are ready to try their hand at a narrative. While the purposes of these two types of essays are very different, the process is essentially the same. In the expository piece, the writers used three objects to create the body of their essay, writing a paragraph about each one. In the narrative essay, three main events of a story make up the three paragraphs.

This fun lesson revolves around an event that has most likely happened to everyone—getting a haircut! (See suggestions at the end of the lesson to adapt this activity to students who have not had a memorable hair cut.) This lesson builds on what was taught in Lesson One and introduces the concepts of brainstorming before beginning to write and using graphic organizers to help plan work.

The idea of creating a graphic organizer for a story is foreign to most children. They often write their stories with little forethought about main events or character development. Students sometimes do not know how their stories will end before they finish writing. This lesson introduces graphic organizers by having students create an organizer for an existing story.

To make this lesson more fun, you may want to introduce your class to three basic kinds of haircuts:

The On-Purpose Haircut. This is the cut at the barbershop or hairdresser or from your grandmother, uncle, or mother while you are in the kitchen or on the back porch.

The Accidental Haircut. Probably familiar to at least one child in the classroom who can remember cutting his own hair with kindergarten scissors.

The Surprise Haircut. This is the haircut that the individual did not intend to get. It may stem from a friend playing beauty salon, a little sister or brother experimenting, or from a classroom experience. The model story in this lesson contains a surprise.

Lesson 2

Prompt Tell about a time that you got a haircut.

Preparation

1. Post the prompt so students can refer to it when they are working. One of the main things students do incorrectly on state assessments is to misinterpret the prompt. Requiring students to use a posted prompt on every lesson will get them in the habit of reading it over and over and thinking about what could go into the essay to address the suggested topics.

2. Copy the model story (page 29) onto chart paper or make an overhead transparency of it.

3. Make one copy of page 30 for each child.

4. Recreate the student graphic organizer from the bottom of page 30 on a piece of chart paper. Include only the + and the four headings.

5. Have on hand two sheets of construction paper for each child.

6. Read aloud the student sample presented on page 27.

Presenting the lesson~Day One

Announce to the class that they will be writing another five-paragraph essay. Point to the prompt you've posted. Read aloud the model story, and ask students to try to identify elements such as the title, the introduction, and the closing. Ask them to point out describing words, where capital letters are used, and when the author indented.

Work as a class to analyze the model story by filling in the blanks on the chart-sized graphic organizer. Use the filled-in organizer on page 29 as your guide. Through this, the students will realize that this story can be summarized, put into three sentences, and placed on a chart.

Now hand out the photocopies of page 30. Ask your students to think about a particular haircut they have had.

Under the section marked "Neat Stuff," students write the answers to these questions:

Was your haircut a surprise, an accident, or on purpose?
Who gave you your haircut?
Where were you when you got your haircut?

Students should think about what they were doing just before the haircut. Were you walking in the mall, playing outside, swimming, getting ready for bed, or were you in school? Write that down where it says "Before."

Think about the haircut. What was it like? How did you feel? Surprised? Sad? Happy? How did the haircut feel? Could you feel a pull or tug? Did the cutter use scissors, electric clippers, or a razor? Did you have your hair washed first? Write one or two things about the haircut where it says "The Cut."

The first thing we do after a haircut is look in the mirror. What did you see when you looked in the mirror? soft, bouncy curls? a bald head? a design? bangs? a burr or a flat top? Did it look good or bad? Where it says "The mirror," write down what it looked like and how you felt.

Discuss, using the suggested questioning techniques, and assist each child in completing the four boxes with information about the story she will be writing. Emphasize to the students that this is just a planning sheet and that the boxes should contain only minimal information and should not be written in complete sentences.

Brainstorm a list of "hair words" that students can use in their essays—trim, cut, curl, razor, shampoo, stylist, barber, for example. This brainstorming session will stimulate creative and descriptive thinking and activate students' prior knowledge. If you post the list, it can be used as a reference for spelling accuracy.

Day Two

Be sure to reread the model, go over the "hair list," and reread the graphic organizers before students begin to write. The writing today will very closely mirror the graphic organizer, so students should have these completed papers on their desks.

Paragraph #1: Writing the Introduction

On the chalkboard or chart paper, write only the words "Snip! Snip!" Ask your students why they think you are beginning your essay this way. Can they think of any other "haircut sounds" that they might want to use for the opening of their story? If they can think of their own (Buzz, Buzz or Clip, Clip, for example), encourage them to use those instead of "Snip! Snip!" Now write the following sentences for the students to copy and fill in the blanks, substituting the words in parentheses as appropriate.

Snip, Snip! (or other sound words) That is the sound of my hair being cut. I will never forget the _____ (day, night, afternoon, morning . . .) that I got my _____ (on purpose, accidental, or surprise) haircut.

Ask students to read this out loud for you. Make sure everyone has indented and written sound words as the first two words of the essay. Remember to "keep them with you" for a while. Continue to circulate and to make suggestions for those who are having difficulty with the sound words. Point to the charts and chalkboard for those who are unsure about spelling.

Paragraph #2: What Happened First?

To begin this paragraph, go straight down under the "s" in the first "Snip" and write "I was just." Instruct students to do the same. This will assure that this paragraph is also indented. Students should then refer to their planning sheet and the box that says "Before." With this information they can finish the sentence, indicating what they were doing before they got their haircut. Each child should write two additional sentences to further indicate their activities and where they were.

Paragraph #3: How Was the Cut?

Now students can refer to the "Hair List" and their graphic organizers to describe the actual hair cut—what was used, how it felt, what the hair looked like, and so on. Encourage them to include at least one feeling or emotion word in this paragraph. A good beginning for this paragraph would be any of the common transition words such as "Then," "Next," "Suddenly," or "Later." Point out that if the haircut was at a salon or barbershop, the name of that place needs to be a capital letter. If they mention the brand names of shampoos or hair sprays, those also have to be capitalized.

Collect the papers at the end of the session.

.* Day Three

Paragraph #4: A Peek in the Mirror...

Hand the students their essays and allow them time to reread and make any changes that they think are necessary.

"When I looked in the mirror . . ." is a good way to begin this fourth paragraph. Put this sentence on the chalkboard, and ask students to include words that indicate what kind of haircut they got (short, buzzed, bald, bangs, a trim) and how they felt about it. What was the reaction of others when they saw the new "do"?

Paragraph #5: Writing the Closing

Brainstorm with students possible beginnings for their closing paragraphs.

I will always remember . . .
I will never forget . . .
That is the story of . . .

After completing this sentence, students should add at least two sentences of their own. Refer to the model or to the student samples for suggestions and ideas.

◆ ◆ ◆ ◆ ◆ ◆ ◆ ◆ ◆ ◆ ◆ ◆ ◆ ◆ ◆ ◆ **TIPS** ◆ ◆ ◆ ◆ ◆ ◆ ◆ ◆ ◆ ◆ ◆ ◆ ◆ ◆ ◆ ◆

- Notice that the graphic organizers used here are numbered 1, 2, 3, and 4. They are placed that way so that the child will later begin to "write in a circle," a concept we will explore in the next lesson.

- If some of your students tell you they have never had a haircut, brainstorm some alternatives with them. Have they had their bangs trimmed or their hair braided? Did they ever get gum or ketchup (or something like that) in their hair, or have they ever worn a special hat? Any of these ideas could make a great story, and they can use the very same graphic organizer and follow the same paragraph beginnings.

Be sure to emphasize the importance of writing an introduction. Tell students that the person reading their essay has not read the prompt like they have. Therefore, they must first "set the stage" for the story to come. In the haircut essay, the student restates the prompt in the opening sentence. Have your students experiment with introducing the prompt without repeating it verbatim.

In the fourth paragraph students tell how they felt about the haircut or how the new "do" made them feel. Interjecting personal emotions into an essay like this is called using "voice." Many state assessments value this ability to personalize writing.

Invite your students to copy the brainstorming lists into their writing folders. As they copy, they can continue to add words that no one else thought of. It is also a good practice in how to spell unfamiliar words. Having the word list in their personal folders makes it easy for them to use this as a reference in future writing too.

◆ *Variations* ◆

If writing about hair doesn't appeal to you, use one of the following prompts for a comparable writing activity.

TELL ABOUT ONE TIME THAT YOU LAUGHED A LOT.

When did it happen, where, and who was involved? (Para. 1 and 5)

Before: What were you doing before you started laughing? (Para. 2)

The Deed: What happened to make you laugh? (Para. 3)

How was it to have such a laugh? What was your reaction? How did others react? (Para. 4)

TELL ABOUT A TIME WHEN YOU LEARNED SOMETHING NEW. Students can think of fun things they have learned to do (ride a bike, learn the rules of a game, take care of an animal).

When, where, and how did you learn something new? Was anyone else there? (Para. 1 and 5)

What were you doing before you learned this great new thing? (Para. 2)

Tell about the new thing. How did you learn to do it? Why did you want to do it? Was it easy or difficult to learn? (Para. 3)

How did you feel about learning this new thing? How did other people react? (Para. 4)

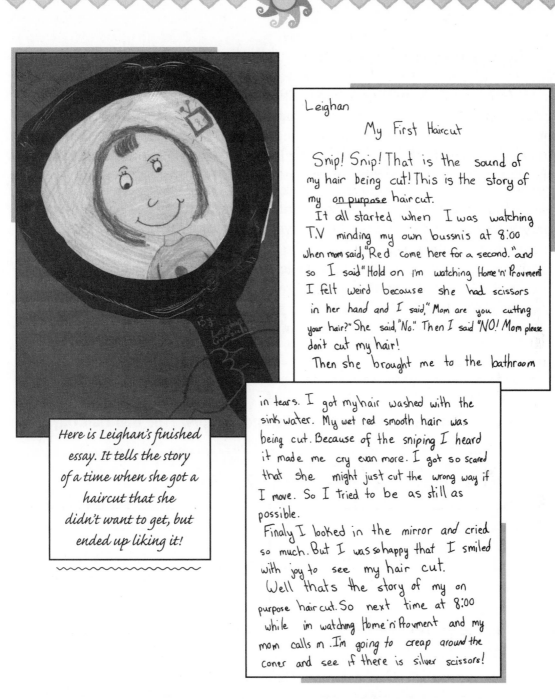

Leighan

My First Haircut

Snip! Snip! That is the sound of my hair being cut! This is the story of my on purpose haircut.

It all started when I was watching T.V minding my own bussnis at 8:00 when mom said, "Red come here for a second." and so I said "Hold on I'm watching Home 'n' Provment I felt weird because she had scissors in her hand and I said," Mom are you cutting your hair?" She said, "No." Then I said "NO! Mom please dont cut my hair!

Then she brought me to the bathroom in tears. I got my hair washed with the sink water. My wet red smooth hair was being cut. Because of the sniping I heard it made me cry evan more. I got so scared that she might just cut the wrong way if I move. So I tried to be as still as possible.

Finaly I looked in the mirror and cried so much. But I was so happy that I smiled with joy to see my hair cut.

Well thats the story of my on purpose haircut. So next time at 8:00 while im watching Home 'n' Provment and my mom calls m .I'm going to creap around the coner and see if there is silver scissors!

Here is Leighan's finished essay. It tells the story of a time when she got a haircut that she didn't want to get, but ended up liking it!

◆ Memorable Hair Cuts Bulletin Board ◆

Give each child an 8" x 12" sheet of black construction paper that has been cut to resemble a mirror. (See illustration.) Have the child draw a picture of himself before, during, or after the haircut and then paste it onto the center of the black circle. Cover pictures with clear plastic wrap. These can serve as a "cover" for the completed story or as part of a barbershop bulletin board display.

◆ *Handwriting Tip* ◆

Most students learn cursive handwriting by the end of third grade. When entering fourth grade, teachers move immediately to traditional lined paper. To make handwriting easier for students, continue to use the three-lined paper that indicates the midline for most lower case letters. This will help the children make the transition to cursive writing much easier.

If students are taking a statewide writing assessment, suggest that they use only manuscript writing unless they are very fluent with their cursive skills. The manuscript usually goes faster, allows the child to concentrate on what she is writing instead of how it looks and how the letters are made, and it usually is easier for the scorer to read, resulting in fewer reader errors due to poor letter formation. Usually just deciphering the fourth grade spelling errors is difficult enough without compounding the difficulty of the situation with poor cursive handwriting.

Graphic Organizer to Use with the model story, "The Bad Hair Day."

I. Neat Stuff ⟶ 2. Before
_____   _____
_____   _____
_____   _____
_____   _____

4. The Mirror ⟵ 3. The Cut
_____   _____
_____   _____
_____   _____
_____   _____

The Bad Hair Day

Snip! Snip! That's the sound of my hair being cut! It all began with a short nap. After that I had a haircut I would never forget.

One day at school I gave my students pieces of gum. There was one piece left, so I began to chew. The problem was that I was still chewing when I lay down on my couch for a short nap.

When I woke up, my hair and face were stuck to a pillow on the couch. I pulled and pulled, but the gum had stuck everything together. I yelled for Mr. Rose to help me. I sat at the kitchen table. He cut and cut, slowly trimming the gum out of my hair.

When I looked in the mirror, one side of my hair was still long and one side was very short. I looked terrible and funny. I had to go to school with crooked hair!

I will never forget that bad hair day. I still take naps after school, but I don't chew gum any more. Can you guess why?

Sample Graphic Organizer for the Model Story:

1. Neat Stuff	2. Before
surprise haircut	at school
Mr. Rose	napping
kitchen	

4. The Mirror	3. The Cut
AHHHH!	gum in hair!
Lopsided	scissors
embarrassed	tangles and pulls

10 Easy Writing Lessons That Get Kids Ready for Writing Assessments
Scholastic Professional Books

Name _____   **Date** _____

Prompt: Tell About A Time You Got A Haircut.

Step One: Under the section marked "Neat Stuff" write the answers to these questions:
Was your haircut a surprise, an accident or on purpose?
Who gave you the haircut?
Where were you when you got the haircut?

Step Two: Think about what you were doing just before the haircut. Were you playing outside, swimming, getting ready for bed, or were you in school? Write that down where it says, "Before."

Step Three: Think about the actual hair cut. What was it like for you? How did you feel? Surprised? Sad? Happy? How did the haircut feel? Could you feel a pull or tug? Did the cutter use scissors, electric clippers or a razor? Did you have your hair washed first? Where was the haircut? In your backyard? At school? At a barber or salon? Write one or two things about the haircut where it says "The Cut."

Step Four: The first thing we do after a haircut is look in the mirror. What did you see when you looked in the mirror? Soft, bouncy curls? A bald head? Bangs? A burr or a flat top? Did it look good or bad? Where it says "The mirror," write down what it looked like and how you felt about the cut.

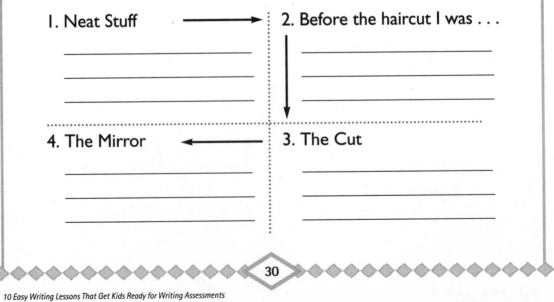

1. Neat Stuff ⟶ 2. Before the haircut I was . . .

4. The Mirror ⟵ 3. The Cut

10 Easy Writing Lessons That Get Kids Ready for Writing Assessments
Scholastic Professional Books

Lesson 3

Writing in a Circle for Effective Endings

Skills Introduced	Alliteration in the title Circle Writing Proofreading that works Writing a closing
Skills Reinforced	Indentation, paragraphing, use of capitals and periods, brainstorming, using a graphic organizer, narrative writing
Time Allotted	Two-to-three 40-minute writing sessions (includes illustrations and display)

Materials	Markers and chart paper for teacher use (about 6 sheets)
	Paper and pencil for students
	Two sheets of white 9" x 12" construction paper for each child (optional)
	Crayons, colored pencils, and scissors for student use

Too often we introduce our students to new concepts without giving them time and opportunity to become good at what we have already taught them. In this lesson, students will pause and practice what they have learned so far. The topic is something that has happened to virtually every child who has reached the age of nine or 10: losing a tooth.

Two new skills are introduced in this lesson: using alliteration and circle writing. These don't come in until the end of the session, long after the student has had time to practice the skills of previous lessons.

When writing assessment scorers refer to a piece as being "whole and complete," they are saying that the writer has exhausted the subject—it has been covered and explained in full or has made the reader feel as if the story is wrapped up and finished. There are many tools for making writing seem whole and complete. One that children can learn to use is called circle writing. To write in a circle, the author simply uses something in the closing paragraph that was mentioned in the introduction. An example of circle writing can be found by looking at the model story in Lesson Two. (Model story introduction: "After that I had a haircut I would never forget." Closing: "I will never forget that bad hair day.") Other examples of circle writing can be found in the model story on page 47; in the sample stories on page 62; and in the essay on page 68.

Alliteration is a fun literary device that is also recognized as a higher-level essay skill. It's easy for students to see the appeal of alliterative names and phrases—would Bugs Bunny be so popular if his name was Greg Rabbit? In this lesson, alliteration will only be used for the title of the story, and it is recommended that this be the very last thing the student does before declaring the piece finished. There have been occasions where students wasted a lot of their writing time trying to think of a title before they began to write. Making sure that the title comes last will prevent this from happening to your test takers!

Lesson 3

Prompt Tell about a time that you lost a tooth.

Preparation

1. Make student copies of the graphic organizer on page 38.

2. Have chart paper (2-3 sheets) and markers ready for use.

Presenting the lesson~Day One

Post today's prompt so that students can refer to it. If a student does have a question—"Can I write about a time that I knocked out my brother's tooth?"—ask her to reread the prompt to decide if that topic fulfills what the prompt is asking you to do. (In this case, the prompt requests that students write about a time when they personally lost a tooth.) Since you won't be able to answer questions for your students when they are taking their state tests, now is a good time to encourage their self-reliance.

Hand out copies of the graphic organizer (page 38). Have students notice the headings that are listed for today's writing. Ask them to think about a time that they lost a tooth: Were they at the dentist? Was it knocked out by an accident? Was it a baby tooth? Which time would they like to write about?

Use the following questions to assist students in completing their organizers:

Neat stuff: Where they were, who else was there, and how old they were they? (Para. 1)

What were you doing *before* the tooth came out? (Para. 2)

Write about the tooth coming out: the blood, the pain, the reaction, the emotion, the hole in the mouth. (Para. 3)

What did you see when you looked in the mirror? Were you happy, sad? Is there a tooth fairy? Is the tooth lost forever? (Para. 4)

Brainstorm a list of "tooth words"—*dentist, pull, ache, floss, blood, fairy.*

Record these terms on the chart paper so that students can use these for references and for spelling accuracy.

Day Two

Writing the Introduction

On the chalkboard, write:

Wiggle, wiggle. That's what I kept doing to my loose tooth.

Students will all write the same opening, but they may choose to use different expressions for the opening two words (*tug, tug; twist, twist; jiggle, jiggle; pull, pull; push, push; tickle, tickle*). Students still need one or two more sentences to make this a complete paragraph. They should be able to look at the box on their organizer marked "Neat Stuff" and find something else to add.

If there is still time in this session after everyone has written an introduction, introduce the opening sentence suggestion for paragraph two:

I was just . . .

You will want to "walk" your class through each of the next three paragraphs, just like in the previous two stories. Do not just write the opening sentence suggestions the board. Do them one at a time, each time making sure that the class is "with you" and not falling behind or dashing ahead. If they become really impatient, ask them to add some describing words or sentences to make their story be more interesting.

Day Three and Four

Just like the haircut story, ask students to copy the sentence opening and finish both the sentence and the paragraph by adding at least two more sentences after the opening one.

Then . . . (Para. 3)
At last I looked in the mirror . . . (Para. 4)

Continue to circulate and observe your students' progress. If your students have thought their stories through and written on their organizers, you should already be seeing improvements. See page 36 to check out the sample of a student's work.

Writing the Closing

Ask your students to reread their introductions out loud, right now. There will be a little bit of noise in the classroom, but it won't last long. Now ask students to think of one word, term or expression that was used in the introduction that they could also use in the closing. Refer to their graphic organizer under "neat stuff" for ideas. The closing might refer to where the child was ("I will never forget that visit to Grandma's house"); to who else was there when the tooth was lost ("Dr. Smith is the best dentist in town"); or to how old they were ("That's what I remember most about kindergarten"). Another way to write in a circle is to mention the first words of the essay: "Now I don't wiggle that tooth any more."

You can ask some students to read their introductions and closings out loud, skipping the three events in the story. You can also read a student's introduction and ask the class to generate ideas to help with a closing. Try to make sure that everyone's closing is more than one sentence long.

Adding a Title

Write a list of familiar alliteratives on the chalkboard or chart paper: Coca-Cola, Rug Rats, Captain Crunch, Tater Tots, Mickey Mouse, for instance. Can students see what the words in these terms have in common? Can students think of any other examples of alliteration?

Explain that alliteration is putting together words that start the same. Now brainstorm some alliterative titles for the tooth stories—Twisty Tooth, Silly Smile, Toothless Tom, Football Fred, that sort of thing.

◆ Variations ◆

TELL ABOUT A TIME WHEN YOU GOT HURT (or SCARED).

- Where, who was there, how old were you? (Para. 1 and 5, Neat Stuff)
- What were you doing before you were hurt or scared? (Para. 2)
- What happened? Be sure to use describing words and emotion words. (Para. 3)
- What happened after you were hurt or scared? Did you go to the hospital? Did the police come? Did you wake up after a dream? How were you rescued? (Para. 4)

(Notice that paragraphs 1 and 5 ask the same questions—this is circle writing.)

Justin

Ouch, Ouch, That is the sound when my tooth came out of my mouth. It started. When I was six years old.

I was just outside with my friend with some toys. Then we played hide and go seek and I had to be it. We got tired of playing that so we started to ride our bikes around the circle real fast.

I started to go to the house and sit down on the

floor and one of my friends was chasing his cousin and fell and his cousin fell on my head and my tooth fell out and I was bleeding. Then I started looking for my tooth that fell out.

Then I told my mom that my tooth came out. So she gave me an plastic bag and put the tooth in it and waited for night time.

Finally at night time I went to bed and put my tooth under the pillow and went to bed. Then I opened one eye

The Tooth Story
by Justin

to see if there is a real fairy in the house trying to get my tooth and giving me money. Then my mom woke me up and looked under the pillow and got $1.00 in the morning and I was happy.

◆ Proofreading Practice ◆

Explain to your students that proofreading is the process of going through their papers looking for mistakes. Have them reread their stories out loud, correcting mistakes as they come to them. Tell them to read very s-l-o-w-l-y and to pay attention to each and every word. By reading out loud slowly and deliberately, they will find words that are repeated, left out, or spelled incorrectly. For a few minutes your classroom will be a little noisy, but you will immediately notice students picking up those pencils and making corrections. What sometimes happens when students proofread is that they see what they think they wrote, not what is actually on the paper.

When they have finished proofreading, discuss what happened. Laugh with them as they volunteer stories about errors that they found in their own work. Remind your students to do this kind of reading on every piece of paper that they are going to turn in to be graded. Allot specific time near the end of writing assignments for them to proofread their work: "I want you to write from 1:00 to 1:20 and start proofreading your work no earlier than 1:20." The quality of their work will improve and this will help eliminate that mad dash to be the first one done on every assignment!

◆ Portfolios ◆

If you have never created portfolios for your class, just collect student work and put it in a file drawer or box. One day, let students help you with passing the work out to the class, so each child can create her own folder. Have students decorate the outside of their folders by making an acrostic of their name or the name of your school, your school mascot, or your town. If you have added dates to the work as part of the page headings, students should be able to put the work in chronological order—a good math lesson!

Do not send too much student work home, unless you include a note requesting that it be returned. Keep student essays throughout the year and use this collection for parent conferences, to show growth, and for student self assessment at the close of school.

◆ Lost Tooth Bulletin Board ◆

Use red construction paper or tissue paper to create a huge pair of lips that are parted and smiling to show teeth. Each child can put a white cover on their tooth story and staple it onto the bulletin board as a tooth.

Student Graphic Organizer
for Tooth Story

1. Neat Stuff ⟶   2. Before

How old were you? _____   I was just . . . _____

Where were you? _____   _____

_____   _____

Who else was there? _____   _____

_____   _____

_____   _____

_____   _____

4. Looking in the mirror ⟵   3. Ouch!

_____   _____

_____   _____

_____   _____

_____   _____

_____   _____

_____   _____

10 Easy Writing Lessons That Get Kids Ready for Writing Assessments
Scholastic Professional Books

Introducing "How-to" Writing

Skills Introduced	Using onomatopoeia Using a carat for additional information Adding vivid description
Skills Reinforced	Indentation, paragraphing, use of capitals and periods, brainstorming, using a graphic organizer, writing in a circle, proofreading, expository writing

Time Allotted	Two-to-three 40-minute writing sessions (includes illustrations and display)
Materials	Markers and chart paper for teacher use (about 6 sheets) Paper and pencil for students Two sheets of black 9" x 12" construction paper for each child (optional) Enough Oreo cookies for each child to have two

By now your students probably know that you can assign them a five-paragraph essay on just about anything! Before introducing new skills, try this fun writing lesson using Oreo cookies. This lesson focuses on expository writing for a process—writing about what must be done first, second, and third to complete a task. The exercise is also designed to help students increase the amount and quality of description in their writing.

This lesson introduces onomatopoeia, the term for words that sound like what they represent: buzz, clap, crack, pop, crackle, and so on. Onomatopoeia used correctly and creatively can help raise test scores. (Since the Oreo lesson involves a lot of description, you might want to try the "Nothing is as good as..." activity on page 45.)

Although the following lesson specifies Oreo cookies, you can substitute many different foods. See Variations on page 44 for suggestions.

Lesson 4

Prompt Tell how to eat an Oreo cookie.

Preparation

1. Purchase enough Oreo cookies so that everyone (including you) will have two cookies.

2. Copy the model story (page 47) onto chart paper or make an overhead transparency of it.

Presenting the lesson ~ Day One

Enter your classroom with a bag of Oreos, and your students' eyes will light up! Tell students that you are going to give one to each of them, but as they eat they will need to help you create a list of all of the words that they can think to describe this particular cookie.

Pass out the cookies with directions not to start eating yet! Ask students what they can tell you about the cookie so far. (It is circular, two colors, bumpy, has designs and words, is in three parts.) Encourage your students to use four of their five senses (taste comes later!). Write each of these observations on your chart paper.

Now ask students to eat the cookie slowly (fifth sense!) and to continue to give you their observations, which you record on the chart.

Instead of "eat," what other words can students think of to describe how cookies are consumed? Add these to your chart too.

Now that the cookies are gone, how were they? Students can reply with any word *except* "good." The cookie might have been delicious, yummy, messy, stale, chocolatey, or any variation of these. Add these words to your chart.

Now is a good time to show your students how to use a delete mark (⎯̉) and carat (∧) to substitute words when they proofread their stories. Write the following sentence on the board:

I ate the cookie, and it was good.

Ask your students to suggest words to substitute for *ate* and *good*. Then edit the sentence using the delete mark and carat:

I ~~ate~~ the cookie, and it was ~~good~~.
(with "devoured" written above *ate* and "delicious" written above *good*)

Also show how the carat can be used alone to add words.

I ~~ate~~ the ∧ cookie, and it was ~~good~~.
(with "devoured" above *ate*, "chocolate" above the carat, and "delicious" above *good*)

Explain to your students that this is a much cleaner way to fix up their essays than crossing out, writing over, trying to erase.

Now present the model story. You might try to act out the story by eating a cookie in the steps described. Point out that each new step is a new paragraph. Ask students to identify and read the various parts of the story. Can they recognize the introduction, the closing, describing words, what happened first? second? third? Can they identify the part that makes it a "circle story"?

Have your students create a graphic organizer for this exercise. Since you will not be giving them word prompts for this essay ("How old were you?" "Where were you?" and such), they can create this organizer by simply listing Neat Stuff (for paragraphs 1 and 5) and the first, second, and third parts of the process (for paragraphs 2 through 4) on parts of a piece of paper. Give students a second cookie, and tell them to eat thoughtfully and slowly, recording each step on the organizer. Work with them as they discover what their "steps" actually are.

Day Two

Writing the Introduction

Now your students should be ready to begin writing their Oreo essays. This time, instead of providing introductory sentences, brainstorm with them to try to come up with a good opener. Take a few suggestions, and write them on the board. Then give your students these options:

They can use an introduction just as you have written it.

They can use an introduction, but change it a little to suit themselves.

They can write their own introduction.

If you want to get the brainstorm rolling, try one of these introductions:

That's the way the cookie crumbles! That's what our teacher said as we bit into our Oreo cookies!

These kids will eat the middle of an Oreo first! That's just what we did today in writing class.

Go over the chart that you made on Day One. Have students pick out words they find especially appealing and list them on their organizers. They should try to use as many of these words as possible to make their story interesting and creative.

Circulate the room as your students work on their essays. Notice how many students understand that each "step" should be a new paragraph (with indentation).

If enough students aren't doing this, you will want to review paragraphing with them. Also see how many of your students using words other than *first, second,* and *third* to begin their paragraphs (*to begin with, next, finally,* and such). Share with the class particularly vivid descriptions you find on students' papers.

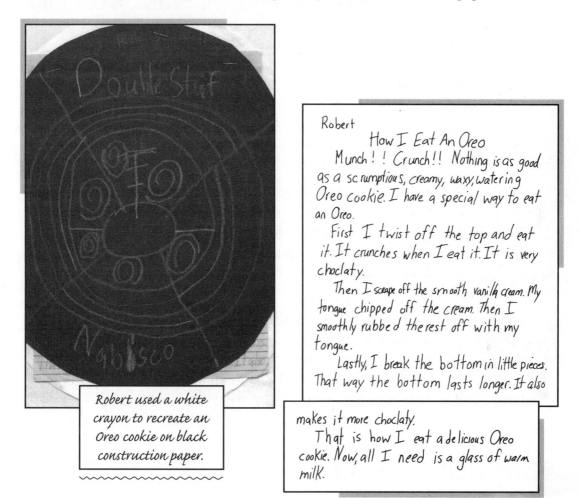

Robert used a white crayon to recreate an Oreo cookie on black construction paper.

Robert

How I Eat An Oreo

Munch!! Crunch!! Nothing is as good as a scrumptious, creamy, waxy, watering Oreo cookie. I have a special way to eat an Oreo.

First I twist off the top and eat it. It crunches when I eat it. It is very choclaty.

Then I scrape off the smooth vanilla cream. My tongue chipped off the cream. Then I smoothly rubbed the rest off with my tongue.

Lastly, I break the bottom in little pieces. That way the bottom lasts longer. It also makes it more choclaty.

That is how I eat a delicious Oreo cookie. Now, all I need is a glass of warm milk.

Day Three

Writing the Closing

If your students did not finish writing paragraphs 2 through 4, let them use the beginning of this session to complete their work.

To get your students started writing their closing, point out circle writing in the model essay. ("Munch, crunch" at the beginning and at the end.) Have students reread their introduction and pick out a way to use something from that paragraph

in their closings. They can refer to their organizers and to the chart of descriptive words for ideas.

Try reading some of their essays or the model out loud. The first time you read, substitute "eat" or "good" for all the descriptive words. Then read the story a second time with the descriptive words in place. Discuss what a difference the addition of describing words makes. Have students practice using a carat to insert or substitute describing words to improve their stories. Then let students trade stories and read their classmates' work.

◆ Variations ◆

There will be at least one child in every class that does not like or cannot eat Oreo cookies or chocolate. You may want to ask your students to vote for their favorite cookies and work with their top two or three choices. Just make sure that you have a variety (a chocolate chip, a peanut butter, and a nonfat, sugar free oatmeal, for instance). You could also do this exercise with a different type of snack food, such as popcorn or pretzels.

Some parents might object to their children eating snacks. Fortunately, this exercise works just as well with fruits, vegetables, or just about any type of food you can think of. Just remember: The word lists and essays will be very different if your students are eating something crispy (such as an apple or celery) or something juicy (like an orange or a tomato).

◆ Oreo Bulletin Board ◆

Have your class create a cookie display using their essay. Each student can make a large "cookie" using construction paper and affix his essay to the cookie. When creating an Oreo, for example, the essay can be the creamy white filling, with two sheets of black construction paper as the chocolate outside. Trim each piece to look like a cookie, and let students add decoration. Display on a tan background with the words "Got milk?" or use bulletin board paper to cut out a large cookie jar. Write "cookies" on the jar and "fill" it with the essays. The jar should be quite large and can be standing up or spilling out across the wall, chalkboard, or bulletin board.

If you do not use cookies for this assignment, modify this activity accordingly (a popcorn bowl, a fruit basket, a salad, or whatever works).

Nothing is as good as . . .

This activity is designed to heighten student awareness of adjectives and how they improve sentences. It is easily done on an overhead or chalkboard. As your students' vocabulary grows, you can repeat this exercise. (Reproducible provided on page 48.)

Nothing is as good as a _____, _____, _____, _____, _ _ _ _ _ _ _ _ on a hot summer day.

Ask students to think of a food or drink that they enjoy on a hot summer day. Write that on the dotted line. Then read the sentence. Now ask them to think of an adjective to describe this food or drink. Add adjectives on the solid lines. Keep rereading the sentence each time you add a new adjective. Repeat this activity with a new food or drink. And another.
Now rewrite it and change it just a little to:

Nothing is as bad as a _____, _____, _____, _____, _ _ _ _ _ _ _ _ on a _____, _____, _____ summer day.

Now ask students to think of things they don't like to eat or drink when it is very hot outside. Can they add more words to describe the summer day too? Remember that the food or drink goes on the dotted line and the adjectives go on the solid lines. Reread the sentence aloud each time you change it.

Vary the sentences by asking students to describe things other than food or drink ("Nothing is as good as a fun game of baseball, a dark sun tan," and so on) or substituting cold winter's night for hot summer's day.

Allow your students to be funny and to enjoy being creative with these sentences.

◆ Adjective Charts ◆

Fold two sheets of chart paper in half and cut along the fold. This will create four long charts. Put one of the following words at the top of each chart:

said   nice   good   fun

Post the charts in a prominent place down low enough that students can continue to add to them. Ask students to think of words that they could use instead of any of these four. Let each child come up and write his word on the correct chart. When a child finds another word that can go on the chart, allow her to add it. When the charts are full, move up the top and tape an additional piece onto the bottom. Can your charts reach from the ceiling to the floor?

◆ Proofreading Practice ◆

In the first proofreading activity, students slowly read their stories to check for meaning. This time ask them to "skim" their stories and look for proper nouns: names of people, towns, stores, or brand names. Remind students that each of those words needs to begin with a capital letter.

Proofreading can be a difficult and lengthy task. If necessary, have students complete their stories one day and proofread the next. They will be reading the story "with fresh eyes" and may find errors that they would have missed had they proofed it at the end of the class time. Do not grade papers until the students have completed proofreading.

If students are having a great deal of difficulty with this, try pairing them and letting them find each other's errors. When pairing students to work together, a good rule is that no one can write on another child's paper. If they find an error, they should point it out to the author, but they should not correct it themselves.

Oreo Fun

Munch, Crunch! Nothing is as good as a round, sweet Oreo cookie. I love the delicious chocolate outside and creamy vanilla inside. I have a special method of eating my Oreos.

First I gently nibble off all of the top cookie. I try not to get any icing on my teeth. I eat all the edges first and the center last.

Then I scrape off all of the icing. It leaves teeth marks that look like roads across the smooth icing. I think this is the best part of the cookie.

Last of all, I eat the bottom cookie. I enjoy this chocolate cookie that turns my teeth black! Sometimes I get crumbs everywhere, but it is worth it.

Now you know how I eat an Oreo. Do you have a special way that is your own? If I give you a cookie, will you tell me about it? Have fun as you munch and crunch your Oreo treat!

10 Easy Writing Lessons That Get Kids Ready for Writing Assessments
Scholastic Professional Books

Nothing Is As Good As . . .

Nothing is as good as a _____, _____,

_____, _____, _ _ _ _ _ _ _ _ _ on a

hot summer day.

Nothing is as bad as a _____, _____,

_____, _____, _ _ _ _ _ _ _ _ _ on a

_____, _____, _____

summer day.

Nothing is as good/bad as a _____,

_____, _____, _ _ _ _ _ _ _ _ _ on a

_____, _____, _____,

cold winter's night.

10 Easy Writing Lessons That Get Kids Ready for Writing Assessments
Scholastic Professional Books

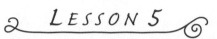

LESSON 5

Adding Expository Elaborations

Skills Introduced	Adding elaborations
Skills Reinforced	Indentation, paragraphing, use of capitals and periods, adding more vivid description, use of carats for insertions, expository essay, proofreading
Time Allotted	Two 40-minute writing sessions
Materials	Scissors for the teacher and for each child Model essay from the first writing lesson Student essays from the first writing lesson Clear tape, one roll for each 4 or 5 students

In this lesson you will use the work that you saved from the first lesson to teach your students to add elaborations to an existing essay. Unlike the previous writing lessons, this one does not involve requiring the students to create a new writing piece.

So far, all the work your students have done would only earn them a middle range score on most writing assessments. This activity is designed to move the student writing up to the higher levels of the scoring rubric. Please do not do this activity before you are sure that your students can independently write a five-paragraph essay with only minimal help from you. If necessary, complete some of the projects listed under Variations (page 18, 26, 35, 44) if you think students need more practice before tackling this important lesson.

Modeling is an integral part of this writing curriculum, and it is absolutely crucial for this lesson. You are going to take the model essay used in lesson one, read it aloud to the class, and then proceed to cut it apart to add "elaborations." Students will then cut apart their own essays, add elaborations, and tape them back together, thus creating "long" stories, a pun that the students find quite amusing. The addition of these "support" paragraphs is what can make the difference between a mediocre and a high score on a writing assessment.

Look at the chart on page 7. There you will find a list of terms commonly used for writing assessment: focus, organization, support, and conventions of print.

Throughout these lessons, our first concern has been **focus**, which is simply getting the student to concentrate and respond to the written prompt. Prompts should have been posted and discussed on each of the three previous lessons. Each of the writing projects so far has been designed to keep students on track and focused.

Organization is one of the hardest things for a nine-year-old child to do. Most adults can sympathize, as most of us are unorganized for at least part of our day! By writing an essay with an introduction, closing, and three ideas in the middle, our students are learning how to organize their thinking before writing. Writing assessment scorers are looking for this kind of organization. However, there are many ways to organize and many ways to achieve a high score on assessments. The five-paragraph essay is not the only way to get there, but it is a great place to start.

Support is the most difficult aspect for students—and perhaps for many teachers—to understand. For the purposes of writing assessments, you may have to erase some preconceived notions about things like elaborations. Students have been using topic sentences in every essay. In the work completed so far, the topic sentence has always been the opening sentence of the paragraph. ("I brought a puzzle piece because I collect antique wooden puzzles.") The extensions are the two sentences that immediately follow that topic sentence. ("Most of them are almost 100 years old. I keep them in heart-shaped boxes.") The extensions serve to support the topic sentence by giving more information about it. Go back now and reread some other five-paragraph essays to identify the topic sentences and the two (or three) extensions that follow. In the examples used here, all of these are pretty obvious.

But now we are talking about elaborations. An elaboration is actually an entire paragraph that serves to support the topic sentence even further. If I added the following paragraph to the original model essay, it would be considered an elaboration of the topic sentence about the puzzle:

My favorite puzzle is the first one I ever bought. I found it at a flea market for only $10.00. It makes a picture of a prancing, white reindeer.

Today's lesson offers some easy ways for students to add elaborations to expository essays. (Information for the narrative elaborations can be found in Lesson Eight.)

Conventions of Print refers to all of those rules and regulations which may drive us crazy, but which also help our writing make sense to the reader. Under the umbrella of "conventions" we would find listed: capitalization, spelling, indentation, and punctuation.

Lesson 5

Preparation

1. In this lesson, you are going to show your students how to add elaborative detail to their work. The technique you will be using involves physically cutting up an essay and affixing separate sheets of detail to the pieces. Prior to

this lesson, you should take the model story you wrote about three things you like and write out details about those things on separate sheets of paper. The day of this lesson, have on hand your model story, a large pair of scissors, some scotch tape, and a staple remover (if the students' papers were stapled). (See teacher sample, page 19. For further clarification, look at the same story that was presented in Lesson One.)

2. Return the essays that students wrote for Lesson One.

3. Have on hand the materials listed at the beginning of this lesson.

4. Read the model essay on page 56 and the student sample on page 54.

Presenting the lesson~Days One and Two

Begin by having students reread their essays. By now they should be capable of recognizing the introduction, the three main topics, and the closing of their stories. Can they explain to you when they started a new paragraph and how that is indicated? Did they know to put proper names in capital letters? Have they used correct punctuation? Many students will want to make corrections in their work. Allow them a few minutes to do so. Celebrate how much they have learned so far this year! Now have students put down their essays and look at yours.

Display your model essay and reread it to the class. Using more than a little flair cut your model apart just after you have talked about your first item (end of second paragraph). Then tape the elaboration you have written about that item onto the bottom.

After taping on the elaboration, tape the cut-off piece back on. Cut again after reading about the second item in your bag. Once again, tape on your elaboration and reattach the rest of the essay. Cut after the third item and add the third elaboration. Reattach the closing paragraph.

Explain to the class that they will be doing something similar to their essays. They are going to cut them apart, tape on some paper, and write elaborations. Then they will tape the paper back together. But they will do it slowly and with your guidance.

To get students thinking about the elaborations they might want to add, create a list of Elaboration Starters. Add to the examples below, and post the list so students can refer to it for future writing assignments.

> **Elaboration Starters**
>
> One time . . .
> The very first . . .
> My favorite . . .
> For example . . .
> The best . . .
> I remember . . .

Assist students in removing staples and finding the first "cutting place" for their essays (just after they have written about their first object or at the end of paragraph two). Now ask students to tape on a piece of blank paper and choose one of the above opening phrases to begin a new paragraph (or to add to the existing paragraph). In this "elaboration" the student gives an example, tells a short story, or gives details about the object he has been writing about. You can help your students by offering suggestions on what they should write about and by allowing students who are ready to read their work aloud. (Be sure they indent, as this is a new paragraph!) When the first elaboration is completed, students will tape their essay back on where they stopped writing.

Ask students to pause and reread what they have written so far. Do they think that the elaboration has helped their story? Were they able to use their good describing skills?

Prepare to cut again! Now the students need to find where they stopped writing about their second object. They will need to cut on that line and tape on some new blank paper. On the newly added paper, students should choose a different phrase from the list and begin to write a detail, a short story, or an example about the second object. When finished, the rest of the story is taped onto the bottom. Students will notice that their stories are becoming quite L-O-N-G!!

Repeat the above steps for the third item, again using a different phrase from the list. When finished, the closing of the essay is taped to the entire long story. Allow students time to read their completed essay in its entirety and to exchange essays with a friend to share their writing.

All About My Life
My name is Carly. I am 9 years old. I think school is cool. In my bag I have three things: my dog tap shoes and a beanie baby.

I brought my dog because I like her. My dog is fun to play with. She is my best friend. My dogs name is Shadow because she follows me around the house. One time when I was playing with my dog and she jumped onto my trampoline. I started to laugh. She started to bark my mom ran to get the camera.

Carly's adds a first elaboration about her dog, shadow.

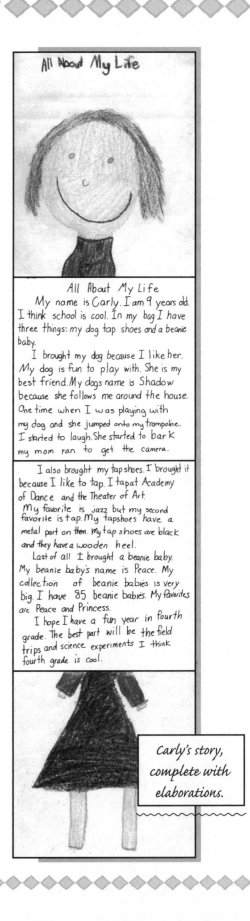

All About My Life
My name is Carly. I am 9 years old. I think school is cool. In my bag I have three things: my dog tap shoes and a beanie baby.

I brought my dog because I like her. My dog is fun to play with. She is my best friend. My dogs name is Shadow because she follows me around the house. One time when I was playing with my dog and she jumped onto my trampoline. I started to laugh. She started to bark my mom ran to get the camera.

I also brought my tap shoes. I brought it because I like to tap. I tapat Academy of Dance and the Theater of Art. My favorite is jazz but my second favorite is tap. My tapshoes have a metal part on them. My tap shoes are black and they have a wooden heel.

Last of all I brought a beanie baby. My beanie baby's name is Peace. My collection of beanie babies is very big. I have 85 beanie babies. My favorites are Peace and Princess.

I hope I have a fun year in fourth grade. The best part will be the field trips and science experiments I think fourth grade is cool.

Carly's story, complete with elaborations.

◆ Variations ◆

Adding elaborative detail is a skill that students should get lots of practice with, so try this exercise with some of the other essays your students have written. Make up different lists of phrases when they add details to their essays about their favorite toys, favorite foods, their haircuts, or losing their teeth.

◆ Long Story Bulletin Board ◆

Students should have created a self-portrait for the cover and should have a blank sheet of paper for the back. Now that the "long" story is complete tape the portrait at the top of the paper and the blank page at the bottom. Have students draw just their feet and legs on the bottom sheet and it will look like a student holding a long sheet of paper in front of his body. (See illustration; page 54.) These can become bulletin board displays, or they can "walk" in the hallways.

Model Essay From Lesson 1 with Elaboration

I have enjoyed being your reading teacher so far this year. I brought this bag to help tell you about me. In the bag I have three things: a puzzle piece, a seashell, and a small book.

I brought a puzzle because I collect antique wooden puzzles. Most of them are almost 100 years old. I keep them in heart-shaped boxes.

(Elaboration Below)

My favorite puzzle is the first one I ever bought. I found it at a flea market for only $10.00. It makes a picture of a prancing, white reindeer.

I also brought a seashell. I brought it because I love to SCUBA dive. Mr. Rose and I go diving one or two times a year. We are careful not to hurt living things under the water.

(Elaboration Below)

One time we were diving at 100 feet deep and I saw a huge manta ray. It was bigger than I am. When it swam by, I was so excited that for a moment, I almost forgot to breathe!

Last of all, I have a book. I brought it because I love to read. Usually I read mysteries. I also read lots of science magazines.

(Elaboration Below)

The best mysteries are by Agatha Christie. I am trying to read all 74 of her books. I especially like the ones that have the Belgian detective, Hercule Poirot.

Now you know three important things about me. We will have lots of fun learning together this year, but first I want to know at least three things about you!

10 Easy Writing Lessons That Get Kids Ready for Writing Assessments
Scholastic Professional Books

Writing Dialogue

Skills Introduced	Using dialogue and quotation marks
Skills Reinforced	Indentation, paragraphing, use of capitals and periods, brainstorming, use of graphic organizer, alliteration, circle writing, proofreading, adding elaborations, expository writing, dialogue and quotation marks
Time Allotted	Two-to-three 40-minute writing sessions
Materials	Markers and chart paper (2-3 sheets) for teacher use Paper and pencils for students

As I've mentioned, this writing program is intended to be a "gradual release" system. Each time your students write, you should give slightly less assistance. You alone know the best pace for your students, and you are aware of when the class is ready to move forward and what areas they need to go over again.

In this lesson students will continue using the skills from the previous lessons and get an introduction to writing dialogue and using quotation marks. You should not expect them to master dialogue writing at this time. Most elementary school students and many middle school students still have difficulty with placing quotation marks, and many teachers discourage students from using them on state writing assessments. Evaluate your students' ability to use quotes, and advise them accordingly for their test situation.

Keep a sharp eye out for all of the elements that the state scorers are looking for. See if your students can be focused and organized and can offer both extensions and elaborations in this writing lesson.

Lesson 6

Prompt Who is your best friend?
Tell why that person special to you.

Preparation

1. Create a chart with sample introductions containing quotation marks. (See samples on page 59.)

2. Have chart paper and a marker available.

2. Read a student sample from the best friend essays on page 61–62.

Presenting the lesson~Day One

Post and discuss the prompt. Explain to students that friends need not only be peers, they can be adults, such as a coach, a minister, a neighbor, even a teacher. Ask students to help you make a list of the qualities of a friend. Record these on a chart and have students come up with examples. (If trust is one of the qualities, then a friend should be someone you can tell a secret to who will not tell everyone else.)

Students should make their own graphic organizers for this essay by dividing a piece of paper into quadrants and writing "Neat Stuff" and the numbers 2 through 4 in those quadrants.

Under "Neat Stuff," each student should record the name of his best friend, his relationship to that person (classmate, coach, piano teacher, neighbor), and where he usually sees that person.

The boxes marked 2, 3, and 4 should each be headed with one of the qualities of a friend that you have listed or with a quality specific to that friend that is not on your chart.

Writing the Introduction

The opening sentence of this essay will begin with a quote, either from the best friend or from the author. Display the chart of quotations, below, on the overhead. Ask your students to suggest some other introductory quotes for this essay. Now have them look at the way the quotes are written. What part is inside of the quotation marks? How can you tell who is talking? How can you tell when they stopped talking? In which openings is the author doing the speaking? (If students have difficulty with this, have half the class read the words in quotes and the other half read the rest of the text and then they can switch jobs.)

- -

"Friends 'til the end!" That is what Marcus and I say about our friendship. Marcus is my very best friend. He lives across the street from me.

"Buddies and Pals!" That is what my I always say to my best friend whenever we say hello or goodbye. Donna has been my best friend for two years.

"Lookin' good!" That is what I always say to my Dad. He is my best friend. I say he is looking good whenever we are playing basketball together.

"Howdy, partner!" That is how my grandfather always says hello to me. He is my best friend in the whole wide world.

"Good morning boys and girls," said Mrs. Rose.
"Welcome to our writing class," beamed Mrs. Rose.
"Ready to write?" asked Mrs. Rose.

Students can choose an opening that is a simple greeting such as some of those listed, or they can use a quote that pertains to friendship ("A friend in need is a friend in deed"). The point here is to understand how to use quotation marks correctly. Circulate the room to make sure that students have indented, made both sets of quotation marks, and included a comma or ending punctuation and sentence ending punctuation. Just getting these openings written may take a while. Assure them that there does not need to be other dialogue in the essay.

Day Two

Students should refer to their graphic organizers to find the first quality they listed for a friend and write at least three sentences about that quality. (See samples of student work on page 62.) After your students have done this, refer to your list of Elaboration Starters. Each student should select a phrase that will be an opening to a good elaboration. Each elaboration should be at least three sentences and should serve to describe an event, situation, emotion, or characteristic related to the friend. You can repeat these steps for paragraphs 3 and 4, but remember: Your students need practice doing this, but you don't want to wear them out! Continue on another day or shorten the assignment if necessary.

Writing the Closing

To write in a circle, students should choose something from the introduction and reuse it in the closing paragraph. (See sample of student work, page 62.) The opening quotation or a variation of it may be used here, or a simple reference to the relationship of the person (uncle, cousin, neighbor, classmate), or even a repetition of the fact that this person is a best friend.

Friends Do Not Fight
By Tim

My friend is Joey. We like the same stuff. We like the same game. We like to play Bond, James Bond. We like it because it has action and girls.

One time Joey and me were playing GoldenEye on Nintendo 64. We almost beat the game. But the boss beat us.

We do not fight because we share our toys. We just don't fight.

For example, we played "Extreme." I won, but I did not brag. We don't talk behind each other's back.

The first time I met Joey I was nine months old. He was one year old.

"Wait up. I want to play too, Joey!"

Tim uses two simple elaborations: "One time" and "for example." He has expanded his skills by learning to use quotation marks.

◆ Variations ◆

1. If you could invite any person, fictional or real, living or dead, to dinner, whom would you invite and why did you choose that person?

2. Who is your favorite family member? Tell why you chose that person as your favorite.

The finished essays should follow this format with the elaborations in place.

Introduction
> First reason why
>> For example . .
> Second reason why
>> I remember . . .
> Third reason why
>> One time . . .

Closing

Michael

"Want some chicken?" That's what I always say to my best friend, Dustin. It's an inside joke!

One reason Dustin is my best friend is because he is fun. We like to ride his mini bike. He has a green honda.

Last saturday we went to the park and we raced. I past him and he crashed and I laughed because he threw his helmet at me.

Dustin and I like the same things. We both like Jaguar cars and racing. We both have quarter midget racecars.

For the last two years we've been

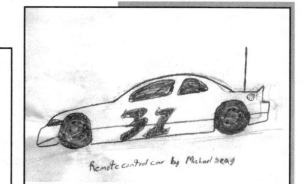

Remote control car by Michael Seay

racing together. It's fun when we pass each other on the track. We both like to win.

Dustin also gives me stuff. One time he gave his remote control car. It was blue and silver and big as some of the ones they race.

When I took it outside it couldn't stop. It got wedged under the tire of his trailer. It left a tire mark on the hood of the car.

Want to hear an inside joke? Ask me or Dustin if we want some chicken. Only best friends know the answer.

Michael's "Best Friend" essay

◆ ◆ ◆ ◆ ◆ ◆ ◆ ◆ ◆ ◆ ◆ ◆ ◆ ◆ ◆ ◆ **TIPS** ◆ ◆ ◆ ◆ ◆ ◆ ◆ ◆ ◆ ◆ ◆ ◆ ◆ ◆ ◆ ◆

- ◆ Try using brightly colored markers to mark the charts that introduce the use of quotation marks. Use red for the quotation marks, green for ending sentence punctuation. Have students underline the parts that are the direct quotes and have them say that part while the teacher reads the rest of the sentence.

- ◆ This is one time that the essay could justify "cleaning up" and editing for correctness. Have students recopy the essays with all corrections made and send them to the person who is the subject of the piece. This can also make a good lesson on how to address an envelope!

Introducing Persuasive Writing

Skills Introduced	Persuasive writing
Skills Reinforced	Indentation, paragraphing, use of capitals and periods, brainstorming, using graphic organizers, circle writing, proofreading, use of the carat, elaborations, using dialogue and quotation marks

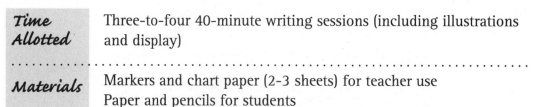

Time Allotted	Three-to-four 40-minute writing sessions (including illustrations and display)
Materials	Markers and chart paper (2-3 sheets) for teacher use Paper and pencils for students Crayons and construction paper (Optional)

In addition to narrative and expository writing, state assessments often require students to write a persuasive essay. In a persuasive essay, the writer attempts to convince the reader to do something or to think a certain way. This is the most difficult kind of writing for young children, and in many states it is not tested until the 8th grade. (See Bonus Lesson for more information on writing an effective persuasive essay.)

The pitfall for many students attempting persuasive essays is that the authors don't include enough information on how the reader will benefit from agreeing with the author's position. Too often students miss the point of persuasion because they tell the reader why they—the authors—like something. ("Going to the beach is the best vacation because I like swimming.") Those types of arguments do nothing to convince the reader that the writer is correct. The effective persuasive essay shows every advantage that the reader will have if he can only act or think the way the writer is suggesting.

This exercise is formatted similarly to the previous essays in this book. This continuity gives students confidence in their abilities and fulfills most requirements for acceptable writing scores. Elaborations are recommended for persuasive essays—after all, good detail helps sell both products and ideas—but if your students are not quite ready to write longer, more involved essays, you don't have to emphasize elaboration at this time.

From this point on I will be presenting the lessons as whole units. You will be better able to determine the pace for your students, and there is no need for me to break down what you should be doing on Day One, Day Two, and so on.

Lesson 7

Prompt Decide which is the better pet, a dog or a cat. Then pretend that you are writing to convince a dog owner that a cat is the better pet, or a cat owner that a dog is the better pet.

Preparation

1. Have chart paper and marker available.

2. Copy the sample introductory paragraph on page 67 onto chart paper.

3. Copy the sample paragraphs onto chart paper or the chalkboard, or have copies to distribute.

4. Read the student sample of this topic found on page 68.

Presenting the lesson

Even if they don't own one, most children have pretty definite feelings about pets. Survey your students to find out how many own dogs or cats, neither or both. Which is the better pet to have? Why? Their reasoning will be both objective ("Dogs can guard your house") and subjective ("Cats are cuter"). After this discussion, post the prompt on the chalkboard.

Generate even more enthusiasm for this topic by creating a chart that has "Woof, Woof!" at the top of one half and "Meow, Meow!" at the top of the other. Ask students to help you list all of the good and bad things about each animal. Record these on the charts along with any special terms that go with that pet (litter box, leash, bark, hiss).

Persuasive writing is a far higher level skill than your students have yet attempted. It might be a good idea to provide your students with the following student examples to give them a better idea of how they should proceed.

To a Cat Owner

One reason you might want to switch to a dog is because they do not use those disgusting litter boxes. *(topic sentence)* Imagine your life without having to clean out that smelly little tray each night! Your whole house will smell better without that mess in one corner of a room. *(two extensions)*

One time I went to visit my cousin and her family. When I first walked in the house, I could smell the litter box. They hadn't cleaned it out for a while because no one wanted to do that nasty job. *(elaboration that further supports the topic sentence)*

To a Dog Owner

Who wants to come home from work and trudge outside in the heat, rain, and snow just to take some dog for a walk? If you switch to owning a cat, you can come home and put your feet up and relax. For just a couple of minutes of cleaning a litter box each day, you won't have to be on a dog's schedule for exercise.

Imagine what your poor pet goes through if you are late coming home. A cat can take care of itself and use the box, while a dog will nervously wait for you and sometimes have accidents on your carpet.

Now the class is probably ready to begin. Have each child make a graphic organizer (four parts of a piece of paper) with the following headings:

Neat Stuff: chosen pet, breed (optional), physical description (para. 1 and 5)
Advantage #1 (para. 2)
Advantage #2 (para. 3)
Advantage #3 (para. 4)

Brainstorm a list of advantages one pet has over the other (a dog barks and a cat doesn't; a dog must be taken out for walks and a cat uses a litter box; a dog likes to play and run and a cat just sleeps). Students should list these ideas and others they come up with on their own in each quadrant of the graphic organizer.

When writing the essay each of these ideas will be developed, and an example will be given as an elaboration.

Writing the Introduction

Put up the chart and read this introduction out loud:

"Woof, Woof!" "Meow, Meow!" What is the sound you want to hear when you open your front door? I think a _____ is the best pet to have, and this paper will convince you to agree with me.

Take a moment here, and ask if students can find the quotation marks. Why are they there? Why are there two separate sets? Then tell students that they may use this introduction and modify it if they want, or they can write their own introductory sentence.

By now students should know how to proceed after their introductions are written. Students should refer to their graphic organizer for the first advantage to owning the chosen pet (the topic sentence), write three sentences about it (extensions), and add detail (elaboration) to further support their premises. (See student sample on page 68.) Remind students to consult the list of Elaboration Starters.

Remind students that what is important here is the topic selection for the three paragraphs. Students will naturally want to list the reasons they like a cat or dog, but this will not convince the reader that it is to his advantage to switch pets. By carefully selecting problems that are caused by the present pet, the writer might just convince the reader to switch.

Writing the Closing

Remind students to write in a circle on this essay. Each child should reread the introduction and come up with something from that paragraph that can be used as a closing. Variations that are similar to or reminiscent of the introduction are also acceptable. Students may want to include another quote. Encourage and help them to do this and to use proper placement of quotation marks.

◆ *Adding the Title* ◆

Because pets are so much fun to have and to write about, suggest that students think of alliterative titles for their essays. Did anyone use alliteration within the essay? Ask those students to read their story out loud so that others can hear the alliteration.

> Meow, meow! Woof, woof! What do you like to hear when you open your front door? I think dogs are the best pets ever!
>
> I think dogs are better because police dogs get bad people that rob banks and steal food and jewelry from stores. Also police dogs get robbers that get in your house.
>
> Dogs some times sleep with you and they are warm and comfy. They are also friendly when they sleep with you. Dogs don't get hair all over

Gabriel writes a very persuasive essay

> the bed like cats do.
> The most disgusting thing about a cat is they make hair balls all over the place and dogs don't do that stuff. Cats eat mise and that is so gross. Dogs don't eat mice.
> Now you know what I like the best. It is a dog!

◆ Variations ◆

Have students write persuasive essays comparing foods or drinks (fruit vs. vegetables, soft drinks vs. juice, hamburgers vs. pizza, and so on).

You can also explore entertainment and recreation topics such as music (rock vs. rap), movies (action vs. comedy), television (why one program is better than another) and sports (baseball vs. football, for instance).

Not all persuasive essays put forth an argument for one thing (for instance dogs) over another (for instance cats). Just as with advertising, some persuasive essays try to convince the reader that something is "the best"—dogs are the best of all pets, baseball the best of all sports, vegetables are the best thing you can eat, and so on. These types of essays are covered in the exercise below on adding elaboration to persuasive essays.

• • • • • • • • • • • • • • • • • • **TIPS** • • • • • • • • • • • • • • • • • • •

You will probably have students who have never owned a dog or a cat and who may not even like animals. These students might want to write instead about a horse, a bird, a fish, or some other kind of pet. They might also attempt to write an essay about why it's a bad idea to have a dog or cat, not why one is preferable to the other. Make it clear to your students that, whatever their personal feelings, they are required to write an essay that satisfies the prompt. They must try to sell the advantages of having a particular pet. On a state writing assessment, students do not have the luxury of rewriting the prompt, and now is a good time for them to see that they might have to put aside their personal experiences and preferences in order to fulfill an assignment.

◆ Dog and Cat Bulletin Board ◆

Create a fun bulletin board by having each child draw a cat or a dog. In the meantime, cut out the letters for "I'm the Greatest!" Ask students to staple their drawings to the bulletin board and to type or print their essays onto "speech bubbles" like those that appear in comics. Finish your display with the dogs facing the cats and their speech bubbles proclaiming their superiority.

◆ Adding Elaboration to the Persuasive Essay ◆

Reproduce and distribute the essay "Classical Music" on page 72. Also copy it onto a chart or transparency.

Essays such as this one on classical music are also persuasive essays, but they are trying to convince the reader that one thing is the best, not just better than one other thing. Advertisers often use this approach to sell products (these cars get the best mileage, this product is the least expense, most effective, and so on).

To convince an audience that a product or idea is the best, you have to sell its merits. Adding good elaboration certainly helps strengthen your argument. In the essay below the student argues the merits of weekend homework. Point out to your class how the student used elaboration to strengthen his case.

◆ *Persuasive Essay Elaborations: Exercise* ◆

Present the following essay to your class and have them add elaborations.

Middle school kids are way too soft. I think there should be a new policy that teachers are required to assign weekend homework of at least two hours' duration. The following ideas are intended to convince our principal that this suggestion has merit.

Weekend homework teaches students how to discipline themselves. Adults do not have the weekends off from work. Many teachers take home papers to grade, and most folks that work in offices work at home too. Many adults even go in to their offices on Sundays just to catch up.

Tests should be given on Mondays only. That way, even if there wasn't any homework, students would have to do some kind of work over the two days off. They should never completely forget about schoolwork anyway. Scheduling all tests on Mondays would also make it easier for teachers to get the papers graded and back to students by Friday.

There is too much free time for middle school students. They are not old enough for jobs and they have too much time to get into trouble. Assigning weekend homework, test studying, and projects would keep them out of trouble. They will thank us if we begin this newest policy.

There are many good reasons to change our homework policy. I have outlined just a few. I hope you have enjoyed reading this proposal and will pass it on to your principal with your own suggestions and examples of why this is such a great idea.

◆ *Challenge!* ◆

If you are teaching an upper level grade, have your class try to write a persuasive essay such as the one on page 70. Give them a statement—for instance, Homework on Weekends Is Good—and have them write an essaying agreeing or disagreeing. Remind them of the importance of adding elaboration to bolster their arguments. As this is a very advanced assignment, you might consider making it a long-range, out-of-class project.

◆ *Proofreading Practice* ◆

Remember to ask students to reread their essay slowly and out loud and to point to each word that they read to see if the story makes sense.

When they are finished, ask them to look at the charts that your class made at the beginning of the writing lesson. Did they use any of these descriptive words? Students who did not use much description, or who want to amend their essays, should go back through their papers and edit them using the carat and delete symbols. Review with them by using the carat to insert at least five adjectives to describe the pet (size words, color words, breeds, actions).

◆ *Handwriting Tips* ◆

Teaching cursive handwriting is always a challenge for teachers of the upper elementary grades. Good handwriting is important on assessments, though—an *o* that looks like an *a* or a *t* that is mistaken for *l* can lower a student's score! When you are presenting lessons like this one, and students are copying directly from the chalkboard, try incorporating a short cursive lesson into the introduction of the essay.

After students have written the first two words of this essay, model good cursive writing on each of the introductory sentences that they will be copying. If necessary, go very slowly, writing only one capital letter and checking the class before finishing the word. If you write letters such as *a*, *d*, or *g*, remind students to "go over the top; stop; put it in reverse and trace back down" to finish the letter. Similarly, when connecting to letters such as *o*, *w*, and *v*, remind them to "stay up near the top of the mid-line." Obviously this can get tedious, so only do it for the first sentence of each paragraph that you are giving them. Then allow students to switch back to manuscript to complete their work. This is not a complete handwriting lesson, but it is a good way to reinforce that others have to be able to read what you have written.

Classical Music

Country, rap, classical, jazz or rock? What kind of music do you like? I think that classical music is the best and that is what should be playing over the intercom system every day at lunchtime.

Classical music soothes your soul. It calms people down and makes them want to listen to it. It has lots of violins so it is smooth and makes people feel relaxed. I think that we would have fewer disruptions in the cafeteria if we played classical music.

(Add elaboration here.)

Other kinds of music are great for parties and fun, but classical music is what belongs in school. By listening to it each day in the cafeteria students would learn to tell the various composers apart and will learn to recognize music that is famous the world over. They might even learn how to match up the music with the time period in which it was written. The right classical music would enhance the learning done in the history classes.

(Add elaboration here.)

Classical music stimulates your imagination too. Most of us first learned about the most famous classical pieces through cartoons. Students could be asked to illustrate cartoons or paintings to match the music they are hearing. It is a good way to infuse the arts into an already crowded curriculum.

(Add elaboration here.)

Please consider my request to play classical music in our lunchroom. Please try it for at least one month and see how the students react. I think they will be calmer, more interested in music and more imaginative. Save the country, rap, jazz and rock for the parties!

10 Easy Writing Lessons That Get Kids Ready for Writing Assessments
Scholastic Professional Books

Classical Music (with elaboration)

Country, rap, classical, jazz or rock? What kind of music do you like? I think that classical music is the best and that is what should be playing over the intercom system every day at lunch time.

Classical music soothes your soul. It calms people down and makes them want to listen to it. It has lots of violins so it is smooth and makes people feel relaxed. I think that we would have fewer disruptions in the cafeteria if we played classical music.

Many studies have shown that music has an effect on behavior. That is why they play the "fight song" at pep rallies and football games. Proper, quiet music will help students behave as if they were in church!

The other kinds of music are great for parties and fun, but classical music is what belongs in school. By listening to it each day in the cafeteria students would learn to tell the various composers apart and will learn to recognize music that is famous the world over. They might even learn how to match up the music with the time period in which it was written. The right classical music would enhance the learning done in the history classes.

One time I was listening to the 1812 Overture and realized that there were cannons being shot off in the middle of the song. The composition is about the War of 1812. There are countless other references to history in our musical heritage.

Classical music stimulates your imagination too. Most of us first learned about the most famous classical pieces through cartoons. Students could be asked to illustrate cartoons or paintings to match the music they are hearing. It is a good way to infuse the arts into an already crowded curriculum.

The best examples of this are in the wedding and funeral marches that are actually parts of famous opera stories. Most classical music that students recognize at all are from cartoons and modern movies.

Please consider my request to play classical music in our lunchroom. Please try it for at least one month and see how the students react. I think they will be calmer, more interested in music and more imaginative. Save the country, rap, jazz and rock for the parties!

10 Easy Writing Lessons That Get Kids Ready for Writing Assessments
Scholastic Professional Books

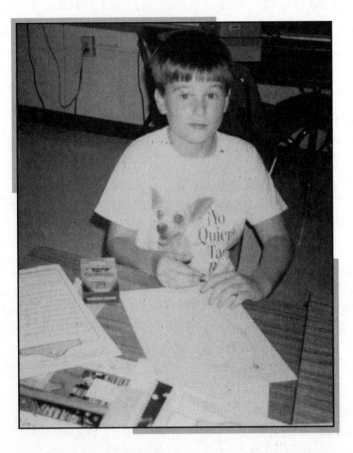

Adding Elaboration to Familiar Stories

Skills Introduced	Adding elaborations to narrative work
Skills Reinforced	Indentation, paragraphing, use of capitals and periods, alliteration, circle writing, proofreading, onomatopoeia, use of the carat, elaborations, using dialogue and quotation marks

Time Allotted	Two-to-five 40-minute time periods (two for this lesson; three more for independent fiction writing within a suggested framework)
Materials	Copy the reproducible stories "The Three Billy Goats Gruff" and "Little Red Riding Hood" so that each student has one; also copy these stories onto chart paper or an overhead transparency. (These are long; the transparency is easier by far!)

In this lesson students begin to stretch their skills beyond the five-paragraph essay by adding elaboration to an existing piece of fiction. Fiction writers use elaboration for a variety of reasons: to describe a scene, an event, a character, or an action; to evoke or explain emotions; to foreshadow or to give background information, and so on. For this lesson, your students will complete two exercises: a whole-group activity adding elaborations to a familiar story and a similar exercise attempted independently.

In the two stories your class will be working on, students are instructed to provide elaboration at certain specific points. Space has been left for them to do so. If they need more room to write, you could have them cut and paste their additions as they did in Lesson Five.

Lesson 8

Preparation
Copy and distribute "The Three Billy Goats Gruff" (page 79) and "Little Red Riding Hood" (page 81); also have these stories on chart paper or an overhead transparency.

Presenting the lesson

1. "Three Billy Goats Gruff"
Read aloud "Three Billy-Goats Gruff," and have your students follow along as you read. (Do not read or refer to the writing prompts at this time.) When you finish, discuss the following with your students and mark them on the chart paper or overhead copy.

- Find examples of alliteration.
- Find examples of onomatopoeia.
- Can you tell who is talking?
- How can you tell when someone new talks?
- Can you read examples of "dialogue" or talk and separate it from text?
- Can you find evidence of circle writing?
- The word *said* is used frequently. What are some more interesting words you can substitute for said?

Now draw your students' attention to the places in the story where they will have to add elaboration. Have them refer to your list of Elaboration Starters. Ask your students why most of these (depending on what you added) are inappropriate for the task at hand. (The Elaboration Starters are personalized—My favorite, I remember, and so on—and will not work in a story that is not about the author.) Explain that you don't need a standard opening to add elaboration. In a piece of fiction, elaboration can be a paragraph that describes a character, setting, or event.

Have your students start reading the story again. Tell them to stop when they get to the prompt for the first elaborations. Here they are asked to describe the troll and the bridge.

Tell your students to close their eyes and picture the scene. What do they see? Is the troll a small, green man with a beard and pointy hat? Is he fat with wispy hair? Could the troll be a woman? How about the bridge? Is it a rickety wooden bridge, or is it stone? Start taking suggestions from your students. Since this is a whole-class exercise, you might want to take elements from different responses—for instance, the troll might be a fat, bearded woman with a wispy ponytail happily sitting at a stone bridge that has holes in it!

> First the youngest Billy-Goat Gruff crossed the bridge. Trip, trap; trip, trap! went the bridge. "Who's that tripping over my bridge?" said a Troll. (Elaboration describes the troll, the bridge.)
>
> **The enormous troll had small green eyes, a wart on his nose and a purple face. He wore ragged clothes made of animal skins. He had long red hair that was matted, tangled and twisting in the wind.**
>
> "It is only I, the tiniest Billy-Goat Gruff. I'm going up to the hillside to make myself fat," said the tiniest Billy Goat in a small voice.

This class added elaboration to describe the troll.

With your students, develop these descriptions into a paragraph. Continue to do this for "Three Billy Goats Gruff" until you have a vividly realized story.

2. "Little Red Riding Hood"

Go over "Three Billy Goats Gruff" with and without the elaborations. Emphasize to your students that elaboration enhances a story, but it does not complete it. "Three Billy Goats Gruff" works perfectly well as a story in its bare-bones format; conversely, if you wrote five paragraphs describing the troll and finished there, "Three Billy Goats Gruff" would no longer have a middle and an ending. All that elaboration would not make up for what was missing to make it a "story" as your students understand it.

Now have your students refer to their copies of "Little Red Riding Hood." As you did with "Three Billy Goats Gruff," discuss with your students use of alliteration, onomatopoeia, substitutions for the word said, and so on.

Read the story aloud, and have your students follow along. Discuss its completeness. Now your students are going to add elaborations to "Little Red Riding Hood." Circulate the room to keep track of everyone's progress. If you notice children getting stuck, you can ask the class for suggestions on a particular area.

When their stories are finished, students can share their work with their classmates. It's as interesting for children as it is for adults to see how people's perspectives are different.

◆ *Variations* ◆

You will probably want to offer your students lots of opportunities to practice this skill. Fortunately it's a fun activity, as students get to visualize stories in ways that are interesting to them. You can use any familiar fairy tale, fable, or folk tale. It's best to use familiar stories so students can concentrate on the elaborations instead of trying to understand the existing text. You can also document simple events ("What we did in science class yesterday") or cut out and copy articles from the newspaper, if they are appropriate.

◆ ◆ ◆ ◆ ◆ ◆ ◆ ◆ ◆ ◆ ◆ ◆ ◆ ◆ ◆ **TIPS** ◆ ◆ ◆ ◆ ◆ ◆ ◆ ◆ ◆ ◆ ◆ ◆ ◆ ◆ ◆

- You may want to consider "blacking out" the elaboration suggestions before you copy "Three Billy Goats Gruff" and "Little Red Riding Hood." They are intended to help students to get ideas, but you may want them to refer to a chart or to think up their own scenarios for elaborations.

- If students are having difficulty with this lesson or if they need more practice in recognizing elaborations, find examples from other familiar fiction. Ask students to point out when the author "paused" and elaborated on a scene, an emotion, or an action. Ask students to find examples in their own personal reading selections.

- If you feel that students need additional practice, try adding elaborations to the tooth story from Lesson Three. It is very easy to further describe pain, appearance of the loose tooth, and the scene of losing the tooth. Remember to cut the story apart and tape it together again as was done in Lesson Five.

- Technically these elaborations create an eight-paragraph essay and should be taught as such. If this is too cumbersome or confusing for some of your students, allow the elaborations to remain within the three main ideas of the essay, thus keeping the five-paragraph format. While this may not be grammatically correct, most state assessment scorers do not deduct for this error.

◆ Punctuation Practice ◆

As your students are working with longer-form material, this might be a good time to remind them about periods and commas. When students are doing their proofreading activities, most of them will "hear" the pauses and know to punctuate. Try some individual help for those who are still having difficulty. When you read stories aloud, be very obvious when you pause for commas and stop at the end of sentences. You can also provide audio clues—tapping the table, lightly for commas, harder for periods—when the child is reading.

◆ Challenge! ◆

There is no shortage of prompts that have been published to encourage students to practice fiction writing. Select one that your students will enjoy, and challenge your class to try their hand at story writing. As a whole-class exercise, have your students write a bare-bones version of a story (introduction, three events, conclusion). They could "fictionalize" a familiar event—a strange visitor to the classroom or a science project gone awry. Then go back and, individually or as a class, add elaboration to "flesh out" the story.

The Three Billy Goats Gruff
(without elaboration)

Once upon a time there were three Billy Goats. All were named "Gruff." They were very hungry. They decided they would cross a bridge to go up to the hillside to eat and make themselves fat.

First the youngest Billy-Goat Gruff crossed the bridge. Trip, trap! Trip, trap! went the bridge. "Who's that tripping over my bridge?" said a Troll. **(Elaboration describes the troll, the bridge.)**

"It is only I, the tiniest Billy-Goat Gruff. I'm going up to the hillside to make myself fat," said the tiniest Billy Goat in a small voice.

"Now I'm coming to gobble you up," said the Troll.

"Oh no! Don't take me. I'm too little. Wait until the second Billy Goat Gruff comes by. He's much bigger."

"Be off with you then!" said the Troll.

After a little while the second Billy Goat came across the bridge. Trip, trap; trip, trap! went the bridge.

"Who's that tripping over my bridge?" said the Troll.

"It is only I, the second Billy Goat Gruff. I'm going up to the hillside to make myself fat," said the second Billy-Goat in a bigger voice.

10 Easy Writing Lessons That Get Kids Ready for Writing Assessments
Scholastic Professional Books

"Now I'm coming to gobble you up," said the Troll.

"Oh no! Don't take me. I'm too little. Wait until the third Billy Goat Gruff comes by. He's much bigger."

"Be off with you then!" said the Troll. **(Elaboration describes the mood of the troll, the pastoral scene on the other side of the bridge, or the approaching Big Billy Goat.)**

Just then, up came the biggest Billy-Goat Gruff. TRIP, TRAP! TRIP, TRAP! went the bridge.

"Who's that tripping over my bridge?" said the Troll.

"IT IS I, THE BIGGEST BILLY GOAT GRUFF!" said the biggest Billy Goat in a huge, loud voice.

"Now I'm coming to gobble you up," said the Troll.

"Well, I've got two spears that will poke your eyeballs out of your ears!" said the Biggest Billy Goat Gruff. He flew at the Troll and poked his eyes out with his horns and crushed him to bits, body and bones. **(Elaboration describes the scene, the action, or the aftermath.)**

Then he went up to the hillside to join his brothers and make himself fat.

10 Easy Writing Lessons That Get Kids Ready for Writing Assessments
Scholastic Professional Books

Little Red Riding Hood

"And give my love to grandmother," said Little Red Riding Hood's mother as she buttoned the cape around her shoulders.

Little Red Riding Hood kissed her mother goodbye and skipped down the walk. Soon she was walking through the forest carrying a basket of good foods for her grandmother. **(Elaboration describes her trip through the forest, the food, the weather, or her mood.)**

Soon Little Red Riding Hood heard a noise. "Chop, chop!" went the loud pounding sound. She had come upon a woodsman who was chopping wood. **(Elaboration describes the scene or the woodsman.)**

He asked where she was going. Little Red Riding Hood told him that she was taking some food through the woods to give to her sick grandmother. The woodsman told her to look out for a big, bad wolf that lived in this part of the forest. "I'll be careful," said Little Red Riding Hood.

When Little Red Riding Hood knocked on the door of her grandmother's cottage, she heard a faint voice telling her to come in. As she entered the cottage, she saw her grandmother in bed, but she could tell something was different. **(Elaboration describes what she sees when she enters the cottage or her mood.)**

"What big eyes you have, Grandmother," said Little Red Riding Hood.

10 Easy Writing Lessons That Get Kids Ready for Writing Assessments
Scholastic Professional Books

"The better to see you with, my dear," replied Grandmother.

"What big ears you have, Grandmother," said Little Red Riding Hood.

"The better to hear you with, my dear," replied Grandmother.

"What big teeth you have, Grandmother," said Little Red Riding Hood.

"The better to EAT you with, my dear," replied Grandmother.

And with those words, Grandmother jumped out of the bed and revealed that she was actually the Big Bad Wolf in Grandmother's nightgown. **(Elaboration describes the wolf's appearance or Little Red Riding Hood's emotions.)**

Little Red Riding Hood screamed and ran from the room. The Wolf chased after her. Just then, the woodsman came into the house. He killed the wolf. **(Add elaboration here.)**

And he helped Little Red Riding Hood find her grandmother who had been tied up outside in a shed. **(Add elaboration here.)**

Grandmother and Little Red Riding Hood thanked the woodsman for saving their lives. Then he went back to chopping his wood. Grandmother and Little Red Riding Hood enjoyed cups of hot tea and some of the delicious cakes that mother had sent. "And mother sends her love too," said Little Red Riding Hood with a smile.

10 Easy Writing Lessons That Get Kids Ready for Writing Assessments
Scholastic Professional Books

LESSON 9

Recognizing the Elements of Good Writing

Skills Introduced	Self-editing and self-evaluation
	Use of simile
	Writing with voice

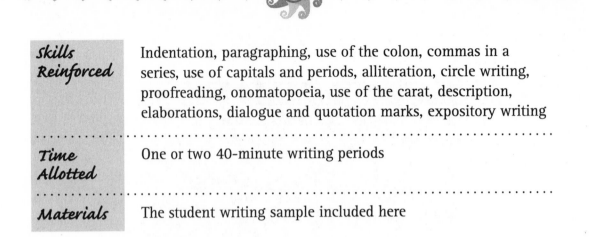

Skills Reinforced	Indentation, paragraphing, use of the colon, commas in a series, use of capitals and periods, alliteration, circle writing, proofreading, onomatopoeia, use of the carat, description, elaborations, dialogue and quotation marks, expository writing
Time Allotted	One or two 40-minute writing periods
Materials	The student writing sample included here

It is important to pause in our instruction and look at what we are teaching our writers. They need to recognize what good writing looks like and learn how to make their own writing even better. This lesson deals with one way to do just that. It begins by looking at a story written by a nine-year-old boy named Vernon. Students look at Vernon's work, identify things that they have been taught, and make suggestions for improving his work. Then students will do the same thing to their own writing and work on some self-editing.

This lesson also reinforces the use of personal feelings, or voice, in an essay and gives a concrete example of the use of a simile. Both of these literary devices can serve to greatly elevate a score on a writing assessment. However, it is very important that the elements of good writing such as similes, voice, description, and alliteration be used appropriately. If the scorer reads an essay in which the child writes, "The stupendous, courageous, marvelous dog ran like a waterfall," the scorer will be pretty sure that the child was copying adjectives from a chart and really did not understand the use of simile. A higher score would be obtained by encouraging the student to write as he would speak, use words with which he is familiar, and avoid devices like simile unless he has mastered them. (Alliteration and onomatopoeia are much easier for young children to understand and use.) Notice that we did not even mention metaphors! Unless a student is a very competent writer, it might be better to avoid them at this point.

Preparation

Reproduce Vernon's story on page 87 on chart paper or an overhead transparency. (This is a long story, but having it on a chart is worth the effort.) You might also make copies of the story for each student to edit along with you. The students can keep these papers for reference.

⋆·* Presenting the lesson

Display the story and ask students to identify things that Vernon has done correctly. As each one is discussed, mark the chart or transparency; better yet, have students come up and circle, underline, or highlight the chart to indicate where the various elements are located.

Your students should notice that Vernon:

◆ used capitals, periods, indented, has five paragraphs

◆ gave first, second, and third reasons that German was his best friend (plays tag, protects me, is kind to me)

◆ had three elaborations (paragraphs beginning with "My favorite," "For example," "One time")

◆ used onomatopoeia (woof, woof) and good adjectives (best, every, high, gently)

◆ wrote "in a circle"

Now ask students to give Vernon advice that can help him to improve his writing. Each time a student makes a suggestion, squeeze it in or use a carat to indicate an addition to the story.

◆ Where could he have used alliteration? (in the title—"Gentle German," "Playful Pal"—or in description such as "flying Frisbee")

◆ Where could Vernon have used a simile? ("runs as fast as lightning," "My dog attacks as quick as a flash.")

◆ Where are some areas that Vernon could have added description? ("His name is 'German' because he is a German shepherd. He is my big, brown and white, hairy best friend" or "When someone enters my yard without permission, my dog perks up his ears, bares his teeth, growls, and attacks.")

◆ Do you think the work could be improved by adding some of Vernon's "voice"— for instance, how does he feel when German protects him? How does he feel when they play together? ("German makes me feel secure." "German makes me feel as if no one can harm me." "I feel relaxed when I am around German.")

◆ How could Vernon have varied his sentence structure? (Instead of "German plays gentle with me," he could use, "With me, German is always gentle.")

◆ Could Vernon have more than one sentence in his closing? What else could he do to further write in a circle? ("Woof, woof! That is the sound of German calling me to go play" or "I am happy to have a dog like German protecting me.")

Just telling students to add description, proofread, or edit is not enough. Working through Vernon's piece gives concrete examples of where, when, and how to improve a piece of writing.

Now select a piece of writing that every student in the class has done. Return these to the students and take them step by step through the entire process listed above, only this time ask students to make improvements on their own papers.

These papers need not be rewritten in their edited form. The real lesson here is having students realize that they can edit their own work.

◆ TIPS ◆

Walk your students through this activity step by step. Keep your class together! If students try to work ahead of you, they might miss the main point of the lesson. When everyone is working on the same piece, students can benefit from the discussion and ideas of others. Also suggest that students refer to the word charts to improve their writing.

If you repeat this activity with another piece of writing or with every child editing a different piece, allow students to pair up and help each other find the elements of good writing and to use what they have learned to improve their work.

Copy (or have students copy) the list below to use as a reference when editing.

Check for capitals, periods	Alliteration
Indented, has five paragraphs	Simile
First, second and third reasons	Voice
Elaborations	Vary sentence structure
Onomatopoeia	More than once sentence in his closing
Good adjectives	
Circle writing	

Good writing and effective essays do not need all of these elements.

Vernon's Dog Story

Woof, Woof! That is the sound of my dog protecting me. His name is German. He is my best friend.

He likes to play tag with me. He chases me every day. My favorite game to play with my dog is racing. I like to race. My dog runs really fast.

German protects me when I'm in danger. He guards my house and my family. If someone hits me, my dog will bite them.

For example, when somebody goes in my yard without permission, my dog attacks. My dog doesn't like people in our yard.

My dog is very kind to me. He doesn't bite me or my family. He doesn't bite my friends either. He plays gentle with me.

One time German and I jumped high in the air to catch a frisbee. I pulled it out of his mouth. He gently gave it back to me.

Now you know the reasons why I say my dog German is my best friend.

10 Easy Writing Lessons That Get Kids Ready for Writing Assessments
Scholastic Professional Books

LESSON 10

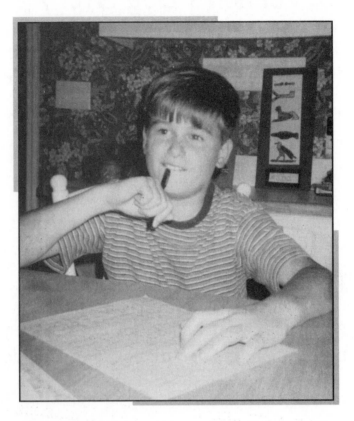

Writing Across the Curriculum

Skills Introduced	Report Writing
Skills Reinforced	Indentation, paragraphing, use of colon, commas in a series, use of capitals and periods, brainstorming, use of graphic organizer, alliteration, circle writing, proofreading, onomatopoeia, use of the carat, adding description, elaborations, dialogue and quotation marks, similes, voice

Time Allotted	Five-to-eight 40-minute writing periods (including illustration and display, but not oral presentations)
Materials	Markers and chart paper for teacher use Reference books related to a subject Paper and pencils for student use Construction paper, crayons, colored pencils (optional, for report display)

The skills that have been taught throughout this book are not just to enhance students' ability to write to a prompt or to raise their writing assessment scores. These are actually life skills. They can very easily be applied to virtually any subject in school. Read through this lesson to see suggestions for ways to use the five-paragraph essay format in report writing, science, social studies, literature, and even math. At the end of the lesson there are suggestions on how to create writing prompts in music, art, and physical education classes. Soon your students will not be dreading those book reports, science projects, and social studies research papers because they will know how to begin, what to look for, how to organize their work, and how to present a completed project for a grade. The bonus? Each writing activity they do in a subject area further strengthens their skills in writing class.

Science

You are nearing the end of a unit on insects. Each student is to choose an insect and write a report about it. All writing must be completed in class.

Step 1: Brainstorming

What could be included in a report about insects? The students list that the report could include:

the home	food	physical description
the habitat	defenses	migration/hibernation
the life cycle	enemies	

Step 2: Getting Started

Each student chooses (or you assign) a different insect to write about and three topics from the list that the class brainstormed. (If it is early in the year or if students have not yet had much experience with the five-paragraph essay format, then you should choose the three topics.) The student can confine his research to these areas about the insect. (For this example the topics will be food, physical description and the home.)

The students create a graphic organizer with quadrants labeled:

1. Neat Stuff   2. Food
4. Home   3. Physical Description

Now the student can begin his research.

Step 3: Research

When students research, they usually find tidbits of information that are interesting but do not really fit into the required report. They cannot resist putting these somewhere into their paper, often where they least belong. This makes the paper seem unorganized and disjointed.

This information can be listed under "Neat Stuff." In this quadrant, students can write down interesting things they learn about the insect that don't fit under the other three headings. For example, the grasshopper spits out "tobacco juice" whenever he is frightened. That piece of information does not belong in any of the other three boxes, but is just too good to leave out of a report.

Students will then look through and read books to find out the rest of their information. When they discover what their insect eats, it goes under the heading "Food." When the student sees a picture and can find out dimensions of the insect, the information goes under "Physical Description." When they find out where the insect lives, they list the information under "Home."

When students are taking research notes, discourage them from writing complete sentences and from copying verbatim out of the book.

1. **Neat Stuff**
   painted lady butterfly
   does not eat
   lives only 4 weeks
   lives in all 50 states

2. **Food**
   proboscis is like a straw
   curls and uncurls
   sucks up flower nectar
   prefers red flowers

4. **Home**
   shrubs, low flowers, yards, parks
   likes flowering trees and vines
   makes chrysalis hanging from the
      bottom of a leaf of a shrub

3. **Physical Description**
   4 Wings
   slender, black body
   3" across
   orange with brown, white and black spots
   black antennae
   black legs

Step 4: Writing the Report

The Introduction

When the student is ready to write the report, he should consult his graphic organizer for ideas. Looking in "Neat Stuff" is usually the best way to find a great beginning. Remind students that they can use any of the introductory ideas that we have used so far: alliteration, onomatopoeia, quotes, questions, or descriptions. (See model essay for example.)

The Body

The body of the report will consist of three paragraphs (based on topics 2 through 4 on the graphic organizer). The student can add elaboration and extensions. (See paragraph 5 of model essay on page 92 for example of elaboration.)

The Closing

Here the student still tries to write in a circle, so that the closing echoes the introduction. It can be the answer to the question, the other half of the quote, a repeat of the noises or movement made by the insect, depending on how he opened his report. (Note that the information in the sample closing did not fit into the other categories, so it was recorded under "Neat Stuff.")

Model Essay

The Butterfly

Look! Quick! Did you just see a butterfly? It just might be the "Painted Lady." It lives in all 50 states.

The Painted Lady butterfly has four beautiful wings. They are orange with specks of brown, white and black. It is only about three inches across its wings. It has a slender black body, long black antennae, and six black legs.

You will find the small butterfly on a shrub or a low flower. Sometimes it lives in flowering trees and vines. It tries to stay near flowers for feeding.

Although the "Painted Lady" lands on flowers, it does not eat them. It does not eat ever! It only drinks the flower nectar. It uncoils its long tongue, called the proboscis, and sucks up the juice. The proboscis is just like a straw!

The "Painted Lady" must visit at least 50 flowers a day to keep itself nourished. It stays only a few seconds, sipping the nectar from the flower and then quickly moves on. In captivity, the "Painted Lady" will drink sugar water from a sponge.

If you see the "Painted Lady" be sure to stop and take a good look at it. They only live about four weeks.

Step 5: Editing and Illustrating

Students should proofread and edit their pieces. Suggest that they pair up and read each other's work and/or read it out loud. They can often find each other's errors. Remind them that if they catch mistakes and fix them, their grades will go up. (Of course, if the teacher finds mistakes, their grade goes down.)

Students will take additional pride in their writing if they know that it will be on display for others to read. Allow time for students to create a bulletin board of their reports, present them to another class, or display them in the library.

You should probably select the topics the first two or three times that students attempt this type of project so that all work is essentially the same. This way you can give group instructions and allow students to develop their skills within a framework.

◆ Science Extensions ◆

Here is a list of report topics and the three supporting paragraphs—the body— that could go with them for similar reports in a science class.

Topic	3-Paragraph Subtopics
electricity	insulators, conductor and circuits
weather	three different kinds of storms (hurricanes, tornadoes, thunderstorms)
geology	three different kinds of rocks (igneous, metamorphic, sedimentary)
chemistry	acids, bases, neutrals
planets	a planet's physical characteristics, its composition and special features it has

Social Studies

The class is studying explorers such as Christopher Columbus. Each student is assigned to write a report on an explorer of her choosing. The students can choose an explorer of any time period: Vasco DeGama, Magellan, Lewis and Clark, Neil Armstrong. The student then follows the same steps for researching and writing her report as she did for the science report.

Step 1: Brainstorm

What could be included in the report? For explorers, a possible list might include:

✓ birth and childhood
✓ places discovered
✓ how he or she died
✓ country represented
✓ how remembered today
✓ years of exploration
✓ most famous for

Robert illustrated his report on Christopher Columbus.

◆ Social Studies Extensions ◆

Remember field trips? Use the same five-paragraph format to write about excursions away from school. The format is the same: introduction, three favorite parts (or three things I saw or three things I learned), and a closing. The essay can easily become an assessment tool gauging the success of the trip and what students actually gained from it.

Topic	Subtopic
Civil War	three causes of the war
An American President	birth/childhood, early political life, famous for
Modern Cities	weather/climate, size/location, fun stuff to do there
Native Americans	food, homes, clothing
Ancient Egyptians	food, homes, clothing

Vroom, Vroom! That's the sound of the Charter buses going to St Augustine. This was going to be the greatest field trip of my life. Also the longest!

The Fort was probably my favorite part of St. Augustine. My favorite place was the gundeck. It gave you the best view of everything. I liked the weapons most.

One of my favorite things were the cannons. Some of the gray ones used to fire up to 1 mile; the green ones used to fire up to 3 miles! I thought the gray ones looked better.

I also liked the oldest wooden school. I thought the bell was very loud, it hurt my ears when it rang! I also liked the wishing well, there weren't many coins in there though.

The robot kid and teacher were my favorite part of the school. I liked how they move and talk. I think they look pretty real.

I liked the blacksmith too. My favorite piece of equipment was the Anvil because on cartoons they always get hit by Anvils. I liked the blacksmiths clothes too. I thought they looked neat.

St. Augustine
By Jeffrey

St. Augustine
by Jeffrey

The part that I liked most was when he was making the nail. I thought it was interesting. how he made it. I know I couldn't ever do that!

Now you've heard my three favorite parts. I hope I go again sometime. Next time I'll bring my camera.

Literature

Consider using the same five paragraph format and writing framework if you are studying biographies.

Step 1: Brainstorming

Make a list of things that you might want to find out about the person who is your subject.

Possible topics:

birth/childhood	where now	adult life
why famous	books written	family
how remembered	education achieved	

Again the student follows the format for researching and writing the report, using all the techniques he has learned to make it interesting for the reader.

◆ TIPS ◆

Writing in a circle has been suggested in every one of these lessons. It is one way for students to make their work seem whole and complete, but it is not the only way. For more experienced writers, it may not be necessary to write in a circle as they may be able to come up with an ending that does not necessarily use ideas found in the introduction.

◆ Sample Prompts for Other Subject Areas ◆

Physical Education

Expository Prompt: Explain how to play the game of tennis.

Narrative Prompt: Tell about the worst game of tennis (or other sport) that you ever played. What happened to make it so awful?

Persuasive Prompt: Your school is going to begin a new sports program. What is the best sport for your school to add to your curriculum, and why is it a good choice?

Music

Expository Prompt: Explain how to sing a song in a "round" format.

Narrative Prompt: Tell about your best (or worst) dance experience ever. What happened to make it so good (bad)?

Persuasive Prompt: What kind of music is best? Persuade your principal to play your choice of music over the loudspeakers at lunchtime.

Art

Expository Prompt: Explain how to make a clay pot without using a potter's wheel.

Narrative Prompt: Tell about a time when you were moved by a painting, sculpture, or other piece of art work.

Persuasive Prompt: Who is the best American artist? Convince the reader that your choice has merit.

Math

Expository Prompt: Explain how centimeters, milliliters, and grams are connected in the metric system of measurement.

Narrative Prompt: Tell about a time when you used the metric system to measure something.

Persuasive Prompt: English or metric? Take a stand on the system that should be used in the United States. Write a letter urging your congressman to use the system you recommend.

Social Studies

Expository Prompt: Tell how Columbus' discovery of America began an exchange of information from one culture to another.

Narrative Prompt: Pretend you are on Columbus' ship. Write about your trip across the Atlantic.

Persuasive Prompt: Was Christopher Columbus' discovery of America a good or bad event? Convince the reader to agree with your opinion.

Science

Expository Prompt: Explain the steps of the water cycle.

Narrative Prompt: Tell about a time when you saw pollution occurring.

Persuasive Prompt: Persuade your friends that littering is a bad thing to do.

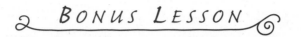

Recognizing Prompts

Time Allotted	Two-to-three 40-minute writing sessions
Materials	Reproducible black line masters for student use

One of the most difficult parts of state writing assessments is determining what kind of writing a prompt is asking the student to do. Is it explanatory, persuasive, or narrative? Many students become confused, which can cause their scores to suffer considerably.

This activity is intended to give students practice determining what kind of prompt they have been given so they will know how to begin planning their essays. Separate prompt practice reproducibles are included at the end of the lesson. Even if your state only assesses one type of writing, it's a good idea for your students to understand how to respond to a prompt.

Some teachers use the terms expository, persuasive, and narrative from the beginning of the school year; other teachers let their students get writing experience before introducing these terms. Whichever method you prefer, there is a secret weapon at your disposal: clue words. Clue words give hints as to what kind of writing the student must do. Teaching your students to always look for clue words will give them an edge when it's time to plan their essays.

◆ *Prompt Practice: Clue Words* ◆

There are certain clue words that help a student determine what kind of essay he will be required to write. If the prompt contains the words "tell how" or "tell why," then the student is being asked to explain something in an expository essay.

If the prompt contains the words "tell what happened," "tell about," or "what happened next," the student should conclude that he has been asked to tell a story, or a narrative, which may be fiction or nonfiction.

Students confuse persuasive essays with expository essays because both involve telling why. In persuasive essays, however, you are not only telling why, you are also convincing the reader to think as you do. Prompts for persuasive essays usually include words such as persuade or convince, and they sometimes mention the audience ("convince your classmates," for instance).

Distribute the reproducible "Making Sense of Prompts" on page 102. Ask students to think about the prompts that you have given them. What kind of essay did they write for the haircut prompt? (narrative) How could they tell? What did they do in that essay? What kind of prompt was the Oreo prompt? (expository) How do they know? What other writing activities have you done this year? Make a list of them and indicate if they were expository or narrative.

When using the "Making Sense of Prompts" reproducible, point out the word *explain*, which is underneath the word *expository*. Students might be able to make a connection by noting the similarity between the two words: If I am explaining, it is expository. Similarly, a narrative essay narrates something. If your students have had experience reading plays, they might be familiar with the role of the Narrator, who is not really a character, but who assists in telling the story. Continue to use "Making Sense of Prompts" while you read and discuss the sample items on page 103. This is a whole group activity which should precede any small group work.

Important Notes About Persuasive Writing

The most important—and perhaps the most difficult—aspect of persuasive writing is recognizing the audience. The student must ask, "Who is going to read this essay?" The obvious answer is "the scorer" or "the teacher," but this is not what is meant by "the audience." The person scoring the essay is actually putting herself in the position of the pet owner, school principal, or other person or group of people being "convinced" by the essay. Once the student figures out who is the intended audience, the rest of the writing goes much easier.

Students need to forget about themselves when writing a persuasive essay. A student writing to persuade the principal to change school rules about the dress code should not offer reasons why this change would make the author happy and how the author would benefit from the new rules. The student must think of ways that the change will benefit the reader of the essay! For example the principal might be impressed if the student convinced him that a new dress code could engender:

- fewer discipline problems

- fewer students in detention for dress code violations

- happier students

- fewer disruptions in class

- additional responsibility for the students to make choices

- less truancy

Certainly these arguments will hold more sway than, "I think the boys should wear neckties every day because I got a really cool tie for my birthday."

As you go through the persuasive prompt exercises, ask students not only to identify the clue words, as is suggested in the narrative and expository prompts, but also to identify the audience. This will put them on the road to writing an acceptable persuasive essay.

Using the Worksheets

The worksheets on pages 103-113 ask students to identify the type of essay called for by a prompt and to pick out clue words. There are two sets of worksheets: One set is for students who will only be tested on narrative and expository writing;

the other set includes persuasive essays. Each set has a sheet for group work and a set for independent work. Answer keys are included for your reference.

Before assigning the independent sheets, it is helpful to have your class work in pairs or small groups. Circulate around the room while students confer among themselves. This peer work can help clarify points for students who aren't "there" yet. Score the exercise with the class, and discuss the answers. When your students are ready, let them work on the second sheet independently. (The sheets ask students to identify the prompt by writing E, N, or P on a line; if your students have difficulty this concept, let them write the words "story," "convince," or "explain" on the lines.)

◆ ◆ ◆ ◆ ◆ ◆ ◆ ◆ ◆ ◆ ◆ ◆ ◆ ◆ ◆ ◆ ◆ ◆ **TIPS** ◆ ◆ ◆ ◆ ◆ ◆ ◆ ◆ ◆ ◆ ◆ ◆ ◆ ◆ ◆ ◆ ◆ ◆

If you are preparing students for a local or state assessment, consider having one or two practice tests about a week before the actual test. Make everything as realistic as you can. When the actual day arrives, the setting and the situations will not be nearly as foreign to your students.

◆ Place the student desks as they will be arranged for the test.

◆ Use the same type of paper that will be used for the assessment and time the students for the very same length of time that the test will take.

◆ Make sure everyone uses the restroom and has sharp pencils.

◆ Allow no interruptions to your classroom. Present the prompts as they will be presented at the test. If they will not be read at the assessment, then don't read them on the practice day.

Caution: Many teachers "over practice." One or two sessions like this should be sufficient for any child. You don't want them to completely stress out over the impending test!

Prompt Practice

1. Everyone thinks his town is a great place to live. Tell why you like living where you do.
Expository. Clue words: "tell why" (so the students give and explain three reasons why their town is a good place to live)

2. You go into your room and shut the door. One of your toys begins to talk. Tell what happens next.
Narrative. Clue words: "Tell what happens next" (so the student tells what happens first, second, and third)

3. It is your room. Tell how to clean it up on a Saturday morning.
Expository. Clue words: "tell how" (the students give step 1, step 2, and so on)

4. You have decided to run for class president. Write a speech to persuade your classmates to vote for you.
Persuasive. Clue words: "write . . . to persuade" Audience: classmates (student should give at least three reasons to vote for him; writer should focus on how voting for him will benefit the classmates, not on reasons why he wants to be president)

5. Suppose you were transported to the days of Robin Hood and "Merry Olde England." Tell a story about an adventure you would have with Robin Hood and his Merry Men.
Narrative. Clue words: "tell a story" (students should tell what happens first, second, and third)

6. Your school recently had to save money, so they cut down on the number of adult crossing guards. Write a letter to your PTA to persuade them to provide funds for more crossing guards.
Persuasive. Clue words: "write...to persuade" Audience: PTA parents (students should give at least three reasons to have crossing guards. Writer should focus on how it will benefit the students and parents of the school)

Making Sense of Prompts

EXPOSITORY
Explain

Clue Words: tell why;
explain

Introduction
First Reason
Second Reason
Third Reason
Closing

Clue words: tell how

Introduction
First Step
Second Step
Third Step
Closing

NARRATIVE
Narrate

Clue Words: what happened
tell a story about
tell about

Introduction
What happened first
What happened second
What happened third
Closing

PERSUASIVE
Persuade

Clue Words: convince,
persuade; also look for hints
for whom to address in the
essay such as principal,
or classmates

Introduction
First Advantage
Second Advantage
Third Advantage
Closing

10 Easy Writing Lessons That Get Kids Ready for Writing Assessments
Scholastic Professional Books

Practice Prompts in Groups
Expository and Narrative Prompts

Read each prompt. If it is asking you to write a narrative (a story that tells happened first, second, and third), put a letter "N" on the line. If the prompt is expository (asking you to explain three reasons why or what to do first, second, and third), put a letter "E" on the line.

Each of these prompts contains clue words that help you know what kind of prompt it is. These will help you get started with your writing. Circle the clue words in each prompt.

1. Almost everyone loves animals as pets. If you could have any pet at all, what would you like it to be and why did you choose that pet?

   _____

2. Everyone has played a game that they will always remember. Choose a game that was special to you and tell why it was special.

   _____

3. Everyone has had funny things happen. Think of one funny thing that has happened to you and tell a story about it. _____

4. Computers are wonderful things. If you could design a computer to do something new for you, what would that something be? Tell why you would choose that task for the computer to do for you.

   _____

5. Most kids in America celebrate birthdays. Tell a story about what happened on your birthday to make it a memorable occasion. _____

6. Your mom tells you to take out the garbage. On the way to the curb you notice a green light all around you. Then you hear a soft whistling sound. Suddenly you realize that you are not alone. What happens next? _____

10 Easy Writing Lessons That Get Kids Ready for Writing Assessments
Scholastic Professional Books

Practice Prompts in Groups
Expository and Narrative Prompts (cont.)

7. Your teacher decided to plant the pumpkin seeds from your Halloween project. When your class returns from the weekend, the plants have grown so much that they have filled your classroom. They begin to grow out of the windows and doors. What happens next? _____

8. Tell how to make your favorite sandwich. _____

9. What if your could have dinner with any person in the world? Whom would you choose and why would you choose that particular person? _____

10. Explain how to play the game Hide and Go Seek. _____

10 Easy Writing Lessons That Get Kids Ready for Writing Assessments
Scholastic Professional Books

Answers for Practice Prompts in Groups
Expository and Narrative Prompts

1. Expository. Explain why you chose that pet to write about. Clue words: "why"

2. Expository. The student should write a short introduction saying what the game was, then three paragraphs telling why that game was memorable. Ends with a closing. Clue words: "tell why"

3. Narrative. Student will write a story (fiction or nonfiction) about a funny event. Clue words: "tell a story"

4. Expository. Student will tell why that task needs to be done. Clue words: "Tell why"

5. Narrative. Student will write a story about a birthday. Usually has introduction, three events (or three parts of one event) and a closing. Clue words: "tell a story about"

6. Narrative. The students will know it is a narration because this event has not happened to them, so the story will be fiction. Clue words: "What happens next?"

7. Narrative. Same reasoning as number 6. Fiction story. Clue words: "What happens next?"

8. Expository. Student should give an introduction and the three steps to sandwich building; should also include a closing. Clue words: "tell how"

9. Expository. Main focus here is to explain WHY that person was chosen. Student should not focus on the dinner, the schedule, or the small talk. Clue words: "why" (indicating that the student should give reasons)

10. Expository. Student should give the introduction, three steps, and closing. Clue words: "explain how"

10 Easy Writing Lessons That Get Kids Ready for Writing Assessments
Scholastic Professional Books

Practice Prompts Independently
Expository and Narrative Prompts

Write an "E" for "Expository" or an "N" for "Narrative" on the line following each of these prompts. Circle the clue words.

1. Explain the proper way to brush your teeth. _____

2. Tell about the saddest day of your life. _____

3. Tell all the steps needed to clean your room. _____

4. Explain why it is important to wear a bicycle safety helmet. _____

5. If you could travel anywhere in the world, where would you like to go? Explain why you chose that particular place. _____

6. What if you woke up one morning and you were a millionaire for a day? Tell a story about you would do for that one day. _____

7. The kids in our school have assignment books. Tell why it is important to write in them every day. _____

8. You go to your desk and find a tiny, smiling mouse inside of it. You don't want to tell the teacher. The mouse talks to you. What happens next? _____

9. Explain how to play the game "tic-tac-toe." _____

10. We are not allowed to chew gum in our school. Tell why this is a good rule to have. _____

10 Easy Writing Lessons That Get Kids Ready for Writing Assessments
Scholastic Professional Books

Answers for Practice Prompts Independently Expository and Narrative Prompts

1. Expository. Clue words: "explain"

2. Narrative. Clue words: "tell about" (Remember that personal narratives can be fiction or nonfiction.)

3. Expository. Clue words: "tell . . . steps"

4. Expository. Clue words: "explain why"

5. Expository. Clue words: "explain why"

6. Narrative. Clue words: "tell a story" (Students should know this is narrative because it is a fictional situation.)

7. Expository. Clue words: "tell why" (If students cannot think of three reasons, tell them to make them up or to use humor to get the point across.)

8. Narrative. Clue words: "what happens"

9. Expository. Clue words: "explain how" (All "how-to" prompts are expository.)

10. Expository. Clue words: "tell why"

10 Easy Writing Lessons That Get Kids Ready for Writing Assessments
Scholastic Professional Books

Name _____   Date _____

Partner(s) _____   _____

Practice Prompts in Groups
Persuasive, Narrative, and Expository

Read each prompt. If it is asking you to write a persuasive essay (intended to persuade the reader to action or convince the reader of something), put a letter "P" on the line. If it is asking you to write a narrative (a story that tells happened first, second, and third), put a letter "N" on the line. If the prompt is expository (asking you to explain three reasons why or what to do first, second, and third), put a letter "E" on the line.

Each these prompts contains clue words that help you know what kind of prompt it is. These will help you get started with your writing. Circle the clue words in each prompt.

1. Almost everyone loves animals as pets. If you could have any pet at all, what would you like it to be and why did you choose that pet?

   _____

2. Everyone has played a game that they will always remember. Choose a game that was special to you and tell why it was special.

   _____

3. Which is better, "paper or plastic"? That is a question you are asked each time you go to a store. Write an essay that will persuade others to make the selection you recommend. _____

4. Everyone has had funny things happen. Think of one funny thing that has happened to you and tell a story about it. _____

5. Computers are wonderful things. If you could design a computer to do something new for you, what would that something be? Tell why you would choose that task for the computer to do for you.

   _____

10 Easy Writing Lessons That Get Kids Ready for Writing Assessments
Scholastic Professional Books

Practice Prompts in Groups
Persuasive, Narrative, and Expository (cont.)

6. Your teacher decided to plant the pumpkin seeds from your Halloween project. When your class returns from the weekend, the plants have grown so much that they have filled your classroom. They begin to grow out of the windows and doors. What happens next? _____

7. Your city has put in a bid to host the summer Olympic games. Write an essay that will convince others that this is or is not a good idea for your town. _____

8. Smaller schools are more personal. Larger schools can offer more varied curriculum. Take a stand on the school size issue and write a letter to the school board that will persuade them to enact a policy supported by your argument. _____

9. Tell how to make your favorite sandwich. _____

10. Your mom tells you to take out the garbage. On the way to the curb you notice a green light all around you. Then you hear a soft whistling sound. Suddenly you realize that you are not alone. What happens next? _____

11. What if you could have dinner with any person in the world? Whom would you choose and why would you choose that particular person? _____

12. Explain how to play the game "Hide and Go Seek." _____

13. Most kids in America celebrate birthdays. Tell a story about what happened on your birthday to make it a memorable occasion. _____

14. You have been selected to move to a new middle school that is just now being built. What would be a good mascot? Write to convince others that your choice is the best one. _____

10 Easy Writing Lessons That Get Kids Ready for Writing Assessments
Scholastic Professional Books

Answers for Practice Prompts In Groups
Persuasive, Narrative, and Expository

1. Expository. Explain why you chose that pet to write about. Clue words: "why"

2. Expository. The student should write a short introduction saying what the game was, then three paragraphs telling why that game was memorable. Ends with a closing. Clue words: "tell why"

3. Persuasive. The student will choose which is better and state that in the introduction. The essay will include three justifications for that choice and end with a closing. Clue words: "persuade others." Audience: store customers

4. Narrative. Student will write a story (fiction or nonfiction) about a funny event. Clue words: "tell a story"

5. Expository. Student will tell why that task needs to be done. Clue words: "tell why"

6. Narrative. The students will know it is a narrative because this event has not happened to them, so the story will be fiction. Clue words: "What happens next?"

7. Persuasive. The call is to convince, since the populace can only form an opinion and cannot act at this time. (Not persuasion to action.) Clue words: "try to convince." Audience: city fathers, mayor, newspaper editor

8. Persuasive. This is also persuasive, but to convince, since the reader will not be the one taking any action. Student should stress how the reader would benefit from the recommended action. Clue words: "that will persuade them." Audience: school board

9. Expository. Student should give an introduction and the three steps to sandwich building; should also include a closing. Clue words: "tell how"

10. Narrative. The students will know it is a narrative because this event has not happened to them, so the story will be fiction. Clue words: "What happens next?

10 Easy Writing Lessons That Get Kids Ready for Writing Assessments
Scholastic Professional Books

Answers for Practice Prompts In Groups
Persuasive, Narrative, and Expository (cont.)

11. Expository. Main focus here is to explain WHY that person was chosen. Student should not focus on the dinner, the schedule, or the small talk. Clue words: "why" (indicating that the student should give reasons)

12. Expository. Student should give the introduction, three steps, and closing. Clue words: "explain how"

13. Narrative. Student will write a story about a birthday. Usually has introduction, three events (or three parts of one event) and a closing. Clue words: "tell a story about"

14. Persuasive. The student is trying to sway opinion. Clue words: "write to convince." Audience: principal, PTA, teachers

10 Easy Writing Lessons That Get Kids Ready for Writing Assessments
Scholastic Professional Books

Practice Prompts Independently
Expository, Persuasive, and Narrative Prompts

Write an "E" for "Expository," a "P" for "Persuasive," or an "N" for "Narrative" on the line following each of these prompts. Circle the clue words.

1. Explain the proper way to brush your teeth. _____

2. Tell about the saddest day of your life. _____

3. Which is the better pet, a cat or a dog? Convince your classmates that your choice is best. _____

4. Tell all the steps needed to clean your room. _____

5. Explain why it is important to wear a bicycle safety helmet. _____

6. Write a letter to your parents persuading them to raise your allowance. _____

7. If you could travel anywhere in the world, where would you like to go? Explain why you chose that particular place. _____

8. What if you woke up one morning and you were a millionaire for a day? Tell a story about you would do for that one day. _____

9. The kids in our school have assignment books. Tell why it is important to write in them every day. _____

10. Rock, Rap, Country, Classical, or Jazz? Write a letter to your teacher that will persuade her to switch to your favorite background music during classroom silent reading time. _____

11. You go to your desk and find a tiny, smiling mouse inside of it. You don't want to tell the teacher. The mouse talks to you. What happens next? _____

12. Explain how to play the game "tic-tac-toe." _____

10 Easy Writing Lessons That Get Kids Ready for Writing Assessments
Scholastic Professional Books

Answers for Practice Prompts Independently Expository, Persuasive, and Narrative Prompts

1. Expository. Clue words: "explain"

2. Narrative. Clue words: "tell about" (Remember that personal narratives can be fiction or nonfiction.)

3. Persuasive. Clue words: "convince." Audience: classmates

4. Expository. Clue words: "tell . . . steps"

5. Expository. Clue words: "explain why"

6. Persuasive. Clue words: "persuading." Audience: parents

7. Expository. Clue words: "explain why"

8. Narrative. Clue words: "tell a story" (Students should know this is narrative because it is a fictional situation.)

9. Expository. Clue words: "Tell why . . ." (If students cannot think of three reasons, tell them to make them up or to use humor to get the point across.)

10. Persuasive. Clue words: "that will persuade." Audience teacher

11. Narrative. Clue words: "what happens"

12. Expository. Clue words: "explain how" (All "how-to" prompts are expository.)

10 Easy Writing Lessons That Get Kids Ready for Writing Assessments
Scholastic Professional Books

Skills to Practice All Year Long

Skills Introduced	Transitional phrases Grabbers and great beginnings
Skills Reinforced	Indentation, paragraphing, capitals and periods, graphic organizers, proofreading, use of the carat, dialogue and quotations, editing, self-assessing
Time Allotted	Varies according to the activity selected
Materials	Varies according to the activity selected

This lesson will give you ideas for activities that can be done any time of the year and in any order. Try using these activities between writing assignments to keep from overburdening students and to keep up their enthusiasm for writing.

• Activity: Assess Students' Knowledge of Print Conventions •

Distribute the reproducible on page 124, or create your own letter welcoming students to your classroom. Reproduce the same letter on chart paper or make an overhead transparency of it.

Challenge students to find the errors in the areas listed. After students have completed the work, let them discuss the errors with a partner or a small group. They can compare and continue to find errors suggested by others. Have students make corrections on the chart paper or transparency.

Answers:
Spelling <u>18</u>
Capitalization <u>8</u>
Punctuation <u>9</u>
Other <u>Indent two times</u>

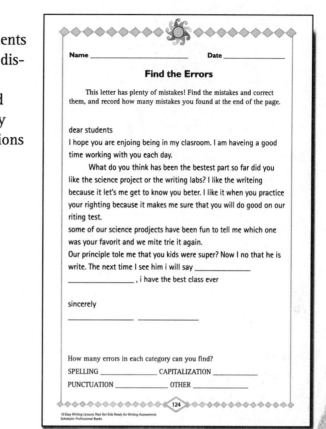

Name _____ Date _____

Find the Errors

This letter has plenty of mistakes! Find the mistakes and correct them, and record how many mistakes you found at the end of the page.

dear students
I hope you are enjoing being in my clasroom. I am haveing a good time working with you each day.
        What do you think has been the bestest part so far did you like the science project or the writing labs? I like the writeing because it let's me get to know you beter. I like it when you practice your righting because it makes me sure that you will do good on our riting test.
some of our science prodjects have been fun to tell me which one was your favorit and we mite trie it again.
Our principle tole me that you kids were super? Now I no that he is write. The next time I see him i will say _____
_____ , i have the best class ever

sincerely
_____ _____

How many errors in each category can you find?
SPELLING _____ CAPITALIZATION _____
PUNCTUATION _____ OTHER _____

124

10 Easy Writing Lessons That Get Kids Ready for Writing Assessments
Scholastic Professional Books

♦ TIPS ♦

If you are teaching older students (fourth grade and up), try giving this assignment at the beginning of the year to get an idea of your class' skill level. You can give similar assignments during the year. Do not grade this paper; use it instead to give students a review and to build their confidence as writers.

◆ *Activity: Identifying Main Events in Literature* ◆

On standardized tests students are often asked to identify the main idea in a story or to summarize the events. Give students an edge by "working backwards," meaning you begin with a finished piece and try to create what the organizer might have looked like when the author began to write. In this lesson, students are asked to think about a familiar story, identify the three main events, and write the events in order on a graphic organizer. This activity helps reinforce the value of planning before you write.

SAMPLE:

Freckle Juice by Judy Blume

Neat Stuff
freckles
school
Sharon is evil character

First
Andrew wants freckles , so he buys a recipe
   that is supposed to give him freckles.

Third
Andrew uses a marker to
   draw freckles on his face

Second
Andrew tries the recipe and gets very sick

Books in the *American Girl* series of historical novels are easy to summarize. Each of these has five chapters: introduction, three "event chapters," and closing. Try creating a graphic organizer for any of these wonderful stories. You can try this activity with any familiar story, fairy tale, even magazine articles.

Three Little Pigs

Neat Stuff
three pigs
new homes of straw, sticks
   and brick
big bad wolf

First
Each pig builds a house

Third
The pigs capture the wolf and
live happily ever after

Second
Wolf blows down the first two houses,
   so the two pigs run to the third house,
   which is made of brick

Have students think back to their haircut and tooth stories. Can they make the connection between the three events in their stories and the way they were planned on the organizer?

◆ *Activity: Tenses and Persons* ◆

Recreate the following sentences on a chart or transparency. Cover the words *past, present,* and *future.*

> **I played on the swings this afternoon. (past)**
> **I will play on the swings tomorrow. (future)**
> **I am playing on the swings today. (present)**

You played on the swings this afternoon. (past)
You will play on the swings tomorrow. (future)
You are playing on the swings today. (present)

They played on the swings this afternoon. (past)
They will play on the swings tomorrow. (future)
They are playing on the swings today. (present)

With the words *past, present,* and *future* covered, ask the students when the activities are taking place. After they have guessed, uncover the answers. Explain what is meant by the term "person." Get your students to assist you in determining which sentences are in first, second, and third person, and use different colored markers to indicate these on your chart.

Continue this exercise using different verbs. Start with verbs that conjugate simply (*walk, walking, walked, walks*) before moving to more complex ones (*swim, swam, choose, chose,* and so on). Work with students so they can identify what person a story is told in, and whether it is told in the past, present or future tense.

◆ *Activity: You Don't Have to Write* The End ◆

Here's a fun way to tap into the artist that's probably hiding in most of your students.

Show your class some magazines that use icons at the end of stories instead of writing "The End." Now have each student create his own icon and use it to "sign" his writing. Soon you will be able to recognize each student's work just by the icon at the end. (Don't let them use popular icons such as the Nike "swoop." Encourage them to come up with something that is unique, original and reflects their own personality.)

Zana Jazzy Carly Tyler Jennifer

◆ Activity: Self-Assessment in Writing Progress ◆

Keeping portfolios of your students' work is an excellent way for both you and them to see progress. Try doing this self-assessment activity at mid year (about January) and repeat it in May.

Duplicate and distribute the self-assessment of writing progress form on page 125. Pass out student portfolios and have each child reread through what she has written so far this year. Ask students to choose what they think was their best piece of writing and the work they are least satisfied with and complete the form.

How I Have Changed as a Writer This Year

Name _____ Date _____

School _____ Grade _____

The piece of writing I am least satisfied with is _____

_____

I am least satisfied with this piece of writing because _____

_____

_____

_____

* *

My best piece of writing so far this year was _____

_____

I think it is my best piece of writing because _____

_____

_____

_____

125

10 Easy Writing Lessons That Get Kids Ready for Writing Assessments
Scholastic Professional Books

◆ Activity: Transition Words ◆

No book on writing would be complete without at least one list of transition words and phrases. These expressions allow us to get smoothly from one paragraph to the other and to "connect" an essay into a coherent piece of work. The problem is that we tend to worry about them so much that it is not unusual for eight- and nine-year-old children to write "in conclusion," "nevertheless," and "furthermore" as they begin paragraphs. This is not the way children talk, and these kinds of transitions make the work feel contrived and unnatural. When students try to use transitions from a chart, quite often they misuse and misplace them.

Students learn best when they work with you to create a classroom list of transition words and phrases. As the list grows, so will their command of grammatical tools. Students can continue to add phrases that they find in their daily reading.

Have your students look through their portfolios to pick out words and phrases they have already used to denote transition. Have them contribute words or phrases to your class list, and discuss their suggestions. (If you have already worked on Lesson Five, you can explain that your Elaboration Starters are transition phrases.) Have your students continue to keep an eye out for transitional phrases as they complete their daily reading and writing assignments. Your list can become quite long!

★ ★ ★ ★ ★ ★ ★ ★ ★ ★ ★ ★ ★ ★ ★ ★

A sample chart from the lessons in this book would include:

I also have	Last of all
I was just	Then
Later	Next
When I	Before I
At last	First
Last	Finally

◆ *Activity: Grabbers and Great Beginnings* ◆

We refer to an exciting opening of an essay or a story as a "grabber" or a "hook." Those great beginnings are intended to keep readers reading beyond the first paragraph or two. Professional authors are very good at getting the attention of the reader and "pulling them in" to continue reading. Bruce Coville says that he likes to mention at least one disgusting body function in the first couple of pages so that the kids who open his books will be hooked. It may seem repulsive to most of us, but it works—kids do keep reading Coville!

Great beginnings and introductions are equally important in student essays, especially if it is for a state assessment. Starting off well shows confidence and a mature level of writing development. Previous writing projects in this book have taught the students to use alliteration, onomatopoeia, quotes, or dialogue as a "grabber." The following activities allow students to get more ideas for introductions by looking at the way professionals get our attention.

★ ★ ★ ★ ★ ★ ★ ★ ★ ★ ★ ★ ★ ★ ★ ★

Quite often teachers give students assignments before they have had enough experience to be successful with the project. Then teachers say that their students "just didn't get it." One very successful model being used around the country today begins with whole group instruction, moves to small group activities, and then finally asks the child to perform independently. Because the child has had so much practice in the whole and small group, the quality of independent work is greatly improved. The activity for Grabbers and Great Beginnings is based on this model. Try using this model for instruction in almost any subject, from math to science to reading. The results will amaze you!

Go over to your bookshelf, randomly pull out a fiction book, and read just the first paragraph or two out loud to your class. See if students can answer the following list of questions from the information on just this first page of the story.

- What do you know about the character?
- What do you know about the setting?
- What kind of book is this? (horror, mystery, romance, science fiction)
- Can you spot any literary devices which you have used in your own writing? (alliteration, onomatopoeia, simile)
- How does the author make you want to keep reading?

Now pass out a fiction book to each pair or small group of students. Ask them to silently read the first paragraph or first page of the book. Have the groups answer questions like those above. Select one student from each group to read the opening paragraphs. Then let that group lead the class discussion of the questions they answered about the story.

Finally, ask students to choose any fiction book from their desks, the library, or your bookshelf, read the opening paragraph, and answer the same list of questions independently on paper.

◆ Extensions ◆

The following activities will give students even more practice in identifying and creating interesting beginnings to stories.

Copy the following sentences onto chart paper or an overhead transparency. Ask students which sentence they think is a better story beginning and why they think so.

My story is about a teacher named Mrs. Rose.
Mrs. Rose laid down her chalk and smiled at her class.

This story takes place at the beach. It is about a girl named Jamie.
The wave rolled right up to the towel Jamie had spread on the sand.

Michael is a football player. He is on a team called the Mustangs.
"Go Mustangs!" shouted the crowd as Michael ran for the touchdown.

In each of the examples above, the second sentence was better. It didn't just give information; it told something about the character or the setting, it helped create a mood, and it made the reader want to know what was going on.

Ask students to listen to the following openings. Can they determine who is the main character and where and when the story takes place? What gives them these clues? (These are great inference questions—a real stumper on many standardized tests!)

Joey climbed into his sleeping bag and gazed up at the stars. He could smell smoke and marshmallows and could see the pale red glow of the fire.
(Joey; camping; night time)

Susan looked at the steep, white mountain spreading out before her. She pulled on her mittens and took a deep breath as she lay down on her belly on the sled. She was shaking, but it wasn't from the cold. "It's now or never," she thought.
(Susan; in the mountains; sledding; cold weather)

Robin pulled back his bow and aimed at the apple on Friar Tuck's head. He was a great bowman, he knew, but could he be good enough not to kill his very best friend and fellow "Merry Man"?
(Robin Hood; Old England)

Ask students to think about the following topics and to name things associated with them. Then see if they can use the items to create opening sentences like the ones in these examples. The opening should give a clue to the character, the setting, or the time period for the story. Topics are listed in bold. Examples are in plain text.

Dogs
leash
bark
water dish
fleas

Witches
broom
black clothes
black cat
potion

Baseball	The Mall
home run	shopping
bat	cashier
uniform	money
cleats	aisle
pitch	shopping bags

Sample opening sentences:

Tommy slid into home plate, hitting his cleat on the catcher' leg.

Susan juggled her shopping bags through the crowded aisles in the shoe department.

The black cat watched as Wicked Matilda slowly stirred her magic potion.

Fido ran around the house with his leash in his mouth.

Repeat this activity throughout the year. Students will get better and better at it. Remind them to use these kinds of openings when they are given independent writing assignments. While these techniques are usually reserved for fiction writing, students can also use these creative ideas for reports in other curriculum areas.

◆ *Activity: Punctuation* ◆

Distribute copies of the Jumping Beans reproducible on page 126. Also have a copy on chart paper or overhead transparency.

Ask students to read the passage and try to determine what has happened in the story. What is the problem here? Why can't you tell who is talking and who said what? What would make it easier to read?

Following the suggestions of your students, go through and add just the periods first. Then put capital letters where they belong on the beginning of sentences. Read the story again. Now it is a little easier to read, but we still don't know when different people start talking.

Work through the passage with students to see where to add the quotation marks, each time stressing that someone starts talking and stops talking. Because people take turns talking, we need to see where they stop and start. Have students read the story, with you reading the teacher part and them reading the student part. Put asterisks to indicate the start of each new paragraph.

The last step, of course, is to add "said the children," and "explained Mrs. Rose" where it is appropriate. Rewrite the passage and have half the class read the teacher part, and the other half of the class read the kids' part and you, the teacher, read the "said ___" parts. Finally, have the students copy this story correctly onto a sheet of paper.

The reproducible on page 127 contains sentences written by fifth grade students. Each sentence contains one error. Distribute this page for your students to practice editing peer work.

Corrections for the Jumping Beans reproducible on page 126:

Mrs. Rose came back in the classroom. "Mrs. Rose, why is that bag moving?" asked the children.
"Oh, that's jumping beans," she replied.
"Those beans got us scared," said the children. "Next time, write the name of what is in it on the outside of the bag."
"I did," explained the teacher.
"Where is it?" the children asked.
"On the other side."
"Well, we were too scared to pick it up and look," exclaimed the students.

Answers for the reproducible on page 127:

1. change were to where; 2. change your to you're; 3. add commas between words in a series; 4. change ever to every; 5. change won't to want; 6. change hear to here; 7. change are to our; 8. remove apostrophe in teacher's; 9. change where to were; 10. add period; 11. change write to right; 12. change their to there; 13. change upper case I in interesting to lower case i; 14. add apostrophe on its; 15. add quotation marks around "I'm sorry."

Find the Errors

This letter has plenty of mistakes! Find the mistakes and correct them, and record how many mistakes you found at the end of the page.

dear students

I hope you are enjoing being in my clasroom. I am haveing a good time working with you each day.

What do you think has been the bestest part so far did you like the science project or the writing labs? I like the writeing because it let's me get to know you beter. I like it when you practice your righting because it makes me sure that you will do good on our riting test.

some of our science prodjects have been fun to tell me which one was your favorit and we mite trie it again.

Our principle tole me that you kids were super? Now I no that he is write. The next time I see him i will say _____

_____ , i have the best class ever

sincerely

_____ _____

How many errors in each category can you find?

SPELLING _____ CAPITALIZATION _____

PUNCTUATION _____ OTHER _____

10 Easy Writing Lessons That Get Kids Ready for Writing Assessments
Scholastic Professional Books

How I Have Changed as a Writer This Year

Name _____ Date _____

School _____ Grade _____

The piece of writing I am least satisfied with is _____

_____

_____

I am least satisfied with this piece of writing because _____

_____

_____

_____

_____

★ ★

My best piece of writing so far this year was _____

_____

_____

I think it is my best piece of writing because _____

_____

_____

_____

_____

10 Easy Writing Lessons That Get Kids Ready for Writing Assessments
Scholastic Professional Books

Jumping Beans

Mrs Rose came back in the classroom Mrs Rose why is that bag moving Oh, thats jumping beans

Those beans got us scared Next time write the name of what is in it on the outside of the bag I did

Where is it On the other side Well we were too scared to pick it up and look

10 Easy Writing Lessons That Get Kids Ready for Writing Assessments
Scholastic Professional Books

Find the Errors

Each of the following sentences was written by a fifth grade student. Each contains one error. Find and correct each mistake.

1. Tell were you live.

2. If your not smart, you won't learn anything.

3. You are a fabulous great super teacher.

4. Ever teacher should try to be kind.

5. If you won't to be kind, bring treats to school.

6. Hear is a joke for you.

7. My teacher lost are papers.

8. Some teacher's are strict.

9. Some kids where mean to me.

10. I'm your new teacher

11. I will grow up write.

12. That's what it is their for.

13. A teacher should be Interesting.

14. Its time for shool.

15. You should say I'm sorry.

10 Easy Writing Lessons That Get Kids Ready for Writing Assessments
Scholastic Professional Books

Conclusion

*H*igher test scores? A fun writing class? Lifelong writing skills? You betcha! This book was not intended to be an "everything you ever wanted to know about writing" book. Indeed many writing skills have been intentionally omitted. But it was intended to give you some expertise on how to break the complicated skill of written composition into its most basic components and to help you hone children's innate abilities to create written pieces on a variety of topics.

I hope this book has proven to be a helpful, simple guide to beginning writing instruction with elementary school students and that you and your classes have enjoyed the activities and have reaped the rewards of higher test scores as a result having done them. From this starting point, students should continue to develop as writers creating far longer, more complicated pieces.

Thank you for all that you do in the classroom—from the first paper bag activity to sweating the test results. Many of us out here appreciate you!